STOCK INVESTING, HOW TO RESEARCH, TRADE EQUITIES, ETFS, AND OPTIONS

Third Edition

ROGER K. DANETH

© Copyright Roger K. Daneth, 2018, 2020, 2021

Important: This book does not advocate the purchase or sale of any particular stock, equity, bond, or other investment. There is risk in stock or equity trading and the investor should be aware of the risks involved. In reading this book, the reader agrees to accept full responsibility for his or her trades regardless of any information, methods, or suggestions presented in this book. This book does not advocate any particular broker, brokerage service, bank, or any other investment or trading service. The advice in this book is intended only to provide knowledge concerning certain methods of stock investing and does not imply that other methods of investing are inferior in any way.

Table of Contents	Section No.
Chapter 1 Can You Beat the Market?	**1.0**
Chapter 2 What to do in a Market Crash	**2.0**
Chapter 3 Checking Stock Fundamentals	**3.0**
What is an Investment?	3.1
Find Statistics on a Stock	3.2
Market Cap	3.3
Enterprise Value	3.4
Trailing Price to Earnings Ratio (P/E)	3.5
Forward Price to Earnings Ratio (P/E)	3.6
Price to Book Value	3.7

Profit Margin	3.8
Return on Assets	3.9
Return on Equity	3.10
Revenue per Share	3.11
Quarterly Revenue Growth	3.12
Quarterly Earnings Growth	3.13
Net Income Available to Common Stock	3.14
Earnings per Share on Diluted Earnings	3.15
Total Cash	3.16
Total Cash per Share	3.17
Total Debt	3.18
Total Debt to Equity Ratio	3.19
Current Ratio	3.20
Book Value per Share	3.21
Operating Cash Flow	3.22
Levered Free Cash Flow	3.23
Beta	3.24
52 Week Change	3.25
S&P 500 52 Week Change	3.26
52 Week High	3.27
52 Week Low	3.28
50 Day Moving Average	3.29
200 Day Moving Average	3.30
Average Volume	3.31
Shares Outstanding	3.32
Shares Float	3.33
Percentage Held by Institutions	3.34
Shares Short	3.35
Short Ratio	3.36
Short Covering	3.37
Program Trading	3.38
Insider Trading	3.39
Gold	3.40
Forward Annual Dividend Rate	3.41
Trailing Annual Dividend Rate	3.42
Five Year Average Dividend Yield	3.43
Payout Ratio	3.44
Dividend Date	3.45
Ex-dividend Date	3.46
Last Split Factor	3.47
Last Split Date	3.48
Chapter 4 Economic Indicators	4.0
Star Indicators	4.1

Federal Reserve Board Indicators	4.2
The Yield Curve	4.3
Weekly Leading Index (WLI)	4.4
Credit Availability	4.5
Purchasing Managers' Index	4.6
London Interbank Rate (Libor)	4.7
TED Spread	4.8
Durable Goods Orders	4.9
Consumer Sentiment	4.10
US National Unemployment Rate	4.11
Tankan Survey	4.12
Housing Starts	4.13
Philadelphia Fed Business Outlook Survey	4.14
S&P 500 PE Ratio	4.15
Crack Spread	4.16
Volatility Index	4.17
TIPS Spread	4.18
US Non-farm Payroll	4.19
Wrapping Up Economic Indicators	4.20
Chapter 5 Trading Methods	**5.0**
Asset Allocations	5.1
Dollar Cost Averaging	5.2
Small Lot Investing	5.2.1
Lump Sum Investing	5.3
Short Term Trading	5.4
Cyclical Stocks	5.5
Day Trading	5.6
Buy and Hold	5.7
401K Plan Investing	5.71
Retirement Plan called an IRA	5.72
Conservative Income Stocks	5.8
High Income Stocks	5.9
New Growth Stocks	5.10
Small Cap Stocks	5.11
Penny Stocks	5.12
Emerging Markets	5.13
Initial Public Offering (IPO)	5.14
High Technology Stocks	5.141
Exchange Traded Funds	5.142
Miscellaneous Investment Categories	5.143
Investment Clubs	5.15
Automated Trading	5.16
Churning	5.17

Re-balancing Your Portfolio	5.18
Chapter 6 Using Options with Stocks	**6.0**
What are Stock Options?	6.1
Covered Calls	6.2
Example of a Covered Call Write	6.3
Writing Put Options	6.4
Buying Puts to Protect Stock Value	6.5

Figures

Fig. 1, Dow Jones Industrial Average since 1900.
Fig. 2, Historical Price of Gold in USD.
Fig. 3, The Credit Management Index.
Fig. 4, The Purchasing Manager's Index.
Fig. 5, Key Durable Consumer Goods Orders.
Fig. 6, US Unemployment rate.
Fig. 7, The Tankan Survey.
Fig. 8, The Crack Spread.
Fig. 9, The VIX vs. the S&P 500.
Fig. 10, The TIPS Spread vs. S&P 500.
Fig. 11, US Non-Farm Payroll.
Fig. 12, Small Cap Stock Fund.
Fig. 13, A Butterfly option spread for the NASDAQ Index.
Fig. 14, An Iron Butterfly option spread for the S&P 500.
Fig. 15, A Condor option spread for the RUSSELL 2000.

Appendix   7.0

1.0 Chapter 1   Can You Beat the Market?

Unless you are a seer or have some kind of sixth sense or psychic powers, it is very unlikely that you can "time" the market--- that is predict ahead of time *when* the market is going to go up or down.

I emphasize the word 'when' because although you can't predict what day, week, or even month, when exactly the market will experience a major correction, you can predict, by studying certain economic indicators, that the economy is moving into an area of uncertainty and possible recession.

We will cover leading economic indicators that are very helpful in making a short- term prediction of an economic downturn. Sometimes you may get a "feeling" that the market does not look good and you should sell out. It is better to be safe than sorry but data shows that people who stay invested all the time, have better gains over long periods of time, on the average. This depends on the quality of your investments however.

If you have gone into very risky stocks or bonds, you may have losses that you will never recover after a major stock market correction. But if you own stock in major high-quality companies, the chances are that these stocks will recover. It is possible to "beat" the market if you define "beat" as doing better than some particular stock index such as the Standard and Poor's 500 index, if you invest in a smart way that gives you good results over a long period of time. By the way, very few mutual funds get better results than the S&P 500.

In this book we will discuss some ways that may give you a chance to at least do well in your investments, if not even get superior results. But remember that I do not guarantee that any particular investing technique I describe in this book will work for you. Your investing results will depend primarily upon your dedication, study, and intelligent application of data to select good investments that will yield good results. You do not have to be a genius or have a Masters degree from Harvard. You only need to understand some basic principles and apply these principles logically and with objectivity.

We will mainly talk about long-term investing as the best way for most investors to get consistently good investment results. Some traders are able to be successful with short term trades, options, or even day trading, all of which methods are a lot more difficult to do and still obtain consistently good results over the long term.

Consider the chart below of the long- term Dow Jones Industrial index price since 1900. Yes, the market can have some temporary deep drops in value, but the long term has been consistently rising in terms of US dollars. Of course, the value of the dollar has also been dropping over the same period of time.

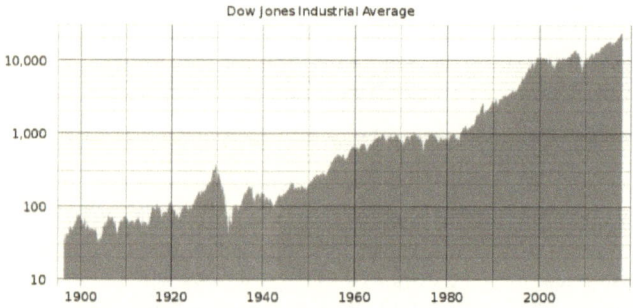

Fig. 1, Dow Jones Industrial Average since 1900.

2.0 Chapter 2   What Should You Do in the Case of a Market crash?

Most investors should always be prepared for a substantial downturn in the market. Your portfolio should be diversified and balanced with high quality dividend paying stocks, stable large capitalization growth stocks, gold, real return funds, investment grade bonds, and other investments that will not be greatly affected adversely by sharp market downtowns.

High technology stocks have been doing very well on the market lately as opposed to the traditional industrial and energy stocks, however don't expect the impressive gains to continue forever.
If you invest in technology stocks, be aware that gadgets and software become obsolete quickly, and new technologies come into play frequently as technical and scientific progress continues. It is also true that there is great opportunity for investors to get in on the latest innovations that will be significant with possible great rewards! As I am writing this, one of the new high technology industries on the scene is the electric vehicle business.

A new class of investments consists of 'crypto currency'. The best example is the digital 'coin', BITCOIN. Crypto currencies are totally virtual in nature. This investment class is quite new in comparison to other investment classes, and it is still quite volatile. There are no physical or metallic versions of crypto coins. One interesting thing about Bitcoin is that the supply is limited and there is great demand. This usually means that the price will increase with time.

Gold tends to retain its value no matter what happens and it is therefore a good hedge against market downturns. I recommend that 5 – 15 % of your portfolio should be invested in gold, especially if there is an indication of inflation ahead. I also recommend keeping 10% or more in cash so you can buy bargains that sometimes develop with market downturns,

There are many methods and theories about asset allocation. I think the best one for the long- term investor is what is known as the "balanced" portfolio that is one where a person has approximately 40% of assets in stocks and 40% in bonds, and in my plan, the rest in gold or some other stable commodity or cash.

 There are also inverse stock funds that generally move in an opposite direction to the market but are very risky to hold over an extended period of time. Also, you could buy put options on stocks that you think might drop quickly in a market downturn. But I have found with experience that buying put options is usually a waste of money or at least a very expensive form of portfolio insurance. We will discuss options in more detail later in this book.

One of the best ways to stabilize your portfolio is with so-called Real Return funds that are practical to hold over the long term and can return you profits if they are traded at the right times. Personally, I like high income stocks that pay cash dividends that are in the 8% to 15% range, as a portion of my portfolio the size of which I can adjust according to my need for income. These kinds of stocks generally do not provide much, if any, capital gain but you can obtain some gain by buying them at the proper times, especially before a dividend is about to be paid. The better high- income stocks also tend to be more stable than stocks that do not pay a dividend because the cash dividend tends to set their base 'value' in terms of the investment yield that they provide.

I can tell you that when the market is declining or is a bear market, it is comforting to see your cash dividends coming into your account on a monthly or quarterly basis. If you do buy high income stocks, try to diversify into various types of high- income stocks, not just bond funds, but also real estate companies like REITS, transportation stocks, energy stocks, telecommunications, energy related sectors, or other industrial stocks that pay high dividends.

If a company pays more than about 6% in dividends it becomes a high- income stock and it is a greater risk in terms of preserving the value of your investment, than stocks that pay 6% or less.

Other kinds of stocks that I like for a stable portfolio are stocks that show a good record of stability during previous market downturns compared to the standard market indexes and other stocks. In this category, I usually choose stocks with excellent fundamentals, large capitalizations, a lot of free cash, growth in sales and earnings, and that have good growth prospects for the future. We will discuss the use of charts and fundamentals in the following chapters to find good stocks.

A lot of people lost money in their 401K plans and IRAs in 2008-2009. Some plans recovered but some did not. Why?

Because the 401K plans that recovered contained high quality stocks or funds, whereas the others that did not had poor quality funds, or even very bad stocks that totally crashed with the market and never recovered.

In 2011, two days after the 513 point crash of the market and the downgrade of USA credit from AAA to AA+, what did I do with my stock portfolio, and what do I plan to do in the future? I did not sell a single stock because all of my stocks are either high quality income stocks or high-quality growth companies. Some of my stocks actually increased in value on the day the market plunged.

Yes, on paper I lost some money in the drop but I am not worried. Why? Because I expect both my high-quality growth stocks and my high-income stocks to recover in price.

I expect my growth stocks to keep growing and eventually be of even higher value in my portfolio. I do not have to try to guess when the market will start to go up again, because I am still invested and as soon as the market starts up again, I will be on the wave at its start.

Yes, the credit downgrade will result in a general increase in interest rates, and the prices of my high-income stocks will drop in price accordingly, but I will still get the good dividends that they provide, sent in cash to my account. (Now in 2021, the Federal Reserve is keeping the interest rates very low. It is a good time to invest in real estate because mortgages are available at low rates.)

In any type of market, bull or bear, I will watch my stocks closely for signs of weakness, major changes in their growth trend, and dividend decreases in my high-income stock portfolio. Dividend decreases happen with high income stocks in any market, so I watch for this and if a stock decreases their dividend to the point that it no longer provides the level of income I want for the money I invested, I will sell it and put the money into a better stock.

Generally, I like high income stocks that pay 10% or higher dividends, preferably on a monthly basis. As I write this, the returns on high income stocks are quite high, and an income investor can do quite well investing in this category. This will not always be the case. In some years, the returns are not that good.

So, if it is a good time to be an income investor and if you try not to sell your shares, you essentially lock-in your dollar returns regardless of what the price of the stock does, as long as the company does not reduce their dividend. Some stocks I have bought have actually increased their dividend which increases my return on my original investment.

Another category of income stocks, are high quality stocks that pay from 2% to 5%, and are increasing their dividends regularly. This category is good for young people that want the possibility of capital gain with increasing income over time.

You always have to watch and track the stocks in your portfolio for negative changes of serious proportions (I don't sell stocks just because their price drops a little), say greater than a 7 or 8% drop. Note that usually just after a high-income stock posts a dividend the stock will decline accordingly in price.

Some people buy a stock just before it goes "ex-dividend" and then sell it immediately after the dividend is paid out. But one last piece of advice on this subject: Don't panic. Stay cool and don't make emotional decisions. Most investors that consistently do well, just sit on their butt, do nothing, and stay invested no matter what the market does.

Now after all of my above comments, if you have been very aggressive and invested in high- risk stocks, and if you get caught in a crash, you may have no choice except to sell your stocks as soon as you can to avoid losing a large portion of your assets.

I do not criticize aggressive investors. Sometimes, or for some personal situations, it may be a good move to be aggressive. But if you are very aggressive, you should have a good understanding of economic conditions so that you are prepared to move out of stocks, hopefully with a capital gain, or move to a less aggressive portfolio, if conditions indicate a possible economic downturn and possibly even a market crash in the near future.

The more aggressive you are, the more you must follow your stocks and the economy, to be ready to sell, buy, or trade. We will discuss economic indicators later.
If you are really risk adverse and don't want the volatility of individual stocks in your portfolio, I recommend looking at Exchange Traded Funds, commonly referred to as ETF's. We will cover these funds in a later section.

3.0 Chapter 3   Checking Stock Fundamentals

Don't skip this chapter because as I talk about the various statistics, I add comments about the market and trading in general that are helpful, especially if you are just starting out in market investing.

3.1 What is an Investment?

My definition of an investment is some kind of property that you invest money into that you have a valid reason to expect that you will obtain some income or capital gain in the future. By the phrase 'valid reason', I mean that you have information of some kind that provides a reasonable or even a high probability that your expectation will come true. The property can be a business, common stock, preferred stock, options, real estate, or intellectual property. Not all property is an investment.

For example, an ordinary family automobile that is used to get groceries and take the kids to school will probably not provide you any income or capital gain in and of itself. However, if it is a vehicle that will be used in a business, or some activity that produces income, then yes, it is part of your investment in that business or activity. It is however an asset that depreciates with time.

An example of something that is not a good investment, is putting money into something that has little or no probability of gain. Examples are buying lottery tickets, feeding slot machines, or most forms of gambling where the odds are heavily against you.

By the way, I try not to think of my personal home as an investment. It is a place to live. I may live in one home for 30 years (I have) and I don't have any plans to move. How much money have I made on my home of thirty years? I don't care because I don't plan to sell it, or rent it out, or refinance it, so it does not earn me any income. I might have a capital gain, but my home is worth more to me than the money I could get for it if I sold it. So, I don't consider my home as an investment.

That is not to say that a home could not be an investment. It could be if I planned to rent it, or remodel it and sell it soon for a profit. Or because of the demographics of the area, it is expected that the value of the home will increase fairly rapidly. Then it is a real estate investment.

3.2 Find statistics on a stock

First of all, we need to talk about stock fundamental statistics. Let's cover some basic ones that are important to start with (You can't have too much information on a stock.) You can find free stock data on websites such as Google and Yahoo finance pages. You could use Google to find other free stock analyses sites--- it should not cost you anything other than time to analyze a stock. When you get on one of the finance stock data pages, type in a stock symbol, such as XOM (Exxon Mobile.) Look for a category link for stock statistics and find statistics such as the ones I describe here.

3.3 Market Cap

Market Cap (market capitalization) is the value of the stock based on the number of shares of stock outstanding and the price that people are willing to pay for it. Note that this is not necessarily what the company is worth. But you can compare this statistic to the next one in the list.

3.4 Enterprise Value

The Enterprise value is a measure of what the stock value is really estimated to be. You can compare this value to the Market Cap and you will see that the company may be over or under valued by the stock price. I usually look for an Enterprise Value that is greater than the Market Cap. The amount that it is greater indicates whether or not the stock is at a bargain price or not.

At the time that I am writing this when oil prices are relatively high, the Enterprise Value on Exxon is a little greater than the Market Cap but only about 1% higher, so the current price of $83 per share is not that great a bargain, but at least it is not overpriced. This company is so well managed however, that a stock hunter might overlook the slight difference and drop the Market Cap from any further consideration.

One thing to note however is that the Enterprise Value is over $400 billion so this is a very large and substantial company that is not likely to go out of business any time soon. Also, since there are a lot of shares outstanding, the market value will be relatively stable compared to stocks with lower capitalization and fewer shares outstanding.

3.5 Trailing Price to Earnings Ratio (P/E)

The Trailing P/E is the measure of what the average value of the price to earnings ratio in the recent past. This number should be compared to the next statistic and it will tell you if the P/E is increasing or decreasing. If it is decreasing it may indicate that the stock is becoming a better bargain or it may indicate that some problem is developing that makes the stock less desirable to investors.

An old rule of thumb is to try to buy a stock when its P/E is less than 10. This may be a good rule for well established industrial stocks like Exxon but it is usually too low a number to expect for a fast- growing technical stock such as some of the new software companies that have come on the scene like Google, Facebook, Amazon, and others.

There is one more area that the rule is a good guide and that is in low-price small cap stocks. Such stocks are usually not well-known and therefore they tend to have a low P/E. I like to invest in this class of stocks because given enough time some of the small cap stocks will ultimately become growth stocks and even become large cap stocks.

But you certainly have to have a long time horizon and have a lot of patience. One method of investing in small cap stocks is to buy an Exchange Traded Fund (ETF). In the ETF a large number of stocks are invested in for a fully diversified fund which reduces the risk for the individual investor. Note that not all ETFs are diversified!

Of course, an ETF investment will not usually produce the rapid growth and large capital gains that an investor might achieve if he or she invests in a great small cap stock that really becomes a winning company in the market place.

3.6 Forward Price to Earnings Ratio (P/E)

A more important statistic is the Forward Price to Earnings Ratio as this statistic tells you what the future P/E is likely to be, and this is really what you want to know. It is however good to compare the trailing and forward P/Es because this is an indication as to whether the popularity of the stock is increasing or decreasing.

A stock's popularity will fluctuate with time depending on the situation and how well the stock is doing at a particular time. In the case of Exxon, at the time I am writing this, the forward P/E is currently less than the trailing P/E. This could reflect the possibility that the price of oil may decline in the near future. Or it could be that people find the stock boring. Or maybe corporate income taxes will be increased.

If you invest in a stock you need to follow the news on the stock and news about the commodity it depends if any. You also need to follow financial news and even general news as a background to your research. By the way, you cannot just buy a stock and forget it. You must do continual research, especially on the stocks you hold as events can develop quickly that can affect the price of your stock.

Getting back to P/Es, you will find by doing a little research that the well-established stocks that do not have high growth rates, will generally sell at lower P/Es than the hot new high technology stocks, or the hot fashionable retail stocks. For example, while Exxon sells at a P/E less than 10 currently, Apple Computer sells at a P/E of over 17.

3.7 Price to Book Value

The next important statistic I look at is the Price/Book value. This statistic tells you how many times above the actual value of a share of the stock you are buying, is worth. In the case of Exxon, currently at a price of 2.67 times the book value of the stock, I claim that the price of the stock is high by this measure, or in other words, it is not a very good bargain.

As they say in real estate, a house is worth what someone is willing to pay for it. So, you should research these questions: Is the fact that Exxon stock is priced this high unusual compared to other stocks of the same industry? Are oil stocks priced high because of the expectation of a rise in the price of oil? Is the high price of the stock reflected by a market that is just priced too high in the first place and maybe it is not a good time to invest in any stocks?

Some stocks you may find are actually priced less than book value. In these cases, caution is also in order because there may good reasons why the stock is priced so low. Maybe the company's earnings are steadily falling or the company is actually losing money, or there is some really negative condition that is prevailing.

By the way, I never even consider buying a stock that is losing money unless there are really good factual reasons that predict good price performance ahead. There is usually just too much uncertainty in this kind of stock. It might keep losing money and eventually file for bankruptcy, or it could eventually become a money-maker.

I would wait until the stock is making money, if it ever does, and then buy it if other statistics look good also, and I want to be in this type of stock. In buying stocks there is always a personal preference. For example, no matter how good a coal mining stock looks statistically, I just don't like coal mining stocks and I don't want them in my portfolio.

The reader will probably also not want to own certain stocks either, no matter how good they look financially. One last comment on price/book value is that some companies make a lot of money but do not have a lot of assets, if they pay out most of their earnings in dividends, or re-invest their earnings into non-tangible assets. In this case, the price/book value might be quite high as they do not hold a lot of tangible assets.

One word of caution: Never buy a stock only because someone whispered it into your ear, or you saw it on a "pink sheet", or everyone is talking about it. Do your own research and get the facts!

3.8 Profit Margin

Profit margin is an important statistic. Profit margin is usually determined mainly by the type of business that the company does. For example, grocery chains usually have low profit margins because the mark-up on regular grocery items is usually only 2% or 3%, whereas an oil stock like Exxon might run 9% or 10% profit margin. Exxon runs at over 9%. Of course, the total amount of money earned is the important measure.

Even at 2% profit margin, a lot of money can be made if the volume of sales is high enough. Profit margin is a good statistic to look at especially if you are comparing similar stocks to each other. It gives you an idea how viable their business is and how efficient the company is in doing their business compared to other similar companies.

3.9 Return on Assets

The Return on Assets is somewhat important depending on the type of business that is being looked at. For example, a bank is likely to have a low return on assets of about 1%, while for a large oil company like Exxon it could be over 10%. It is a good statistic to compare companies in the same industry, but not to compare stocks between industries.

It means how much money a company makes on the physical assets that they hold or control. It could be commodities like gold, silver, copper, oil, wheat, treasury bonds, stocks, money funds, or other types of assets. In a general sense, I like to see both a good return on assets (ROA), and a good return on equity (ROE), with the latter being the more important.

3.10 Return on Equity

Return on Equity (ROE) is one of the most important statistics in evaluating a company's stock quality. I like to see a return on equity of at least 15% or better. This is a measure of how much money the stock returns to investors on their investments in the company, on the average.

This statistic immediately gives you an idea how much return you will most likely receive over the long term when you invest in the company. This includes increases in the price of the shares, dividends, etc. The value of 15%, compares across industries, so any stock you are thinking of investing in should have a return on equity of at least 15%.

For Exxon, the return on equity is listed as almost 26% currently as I am writing this book. Of course, you should not use only this statistic in judging a stock. You should consider all available statistics, news, financial reports, analyst ratings, past performance (charts), management age, and whether they are buying or selling stock (insider trading) in their company and what percent of the outstanding stock, management actually owns.

While we are talking about other factors, I should mention another one, and that is whether institutions are buying or selling the stock, or even own any of the stock. By the way, institutions and professional investors usually do not even consider buying stocks that are listed at less than $10 a share.

Sometimes, a stock that is selling for less than $10 can suffer a reverse split, for example if you held 100 shares of the stock you could suddenly own only 10 shares. Yes, this would result in an immediate increase in the price of the stock, but it could then easily decline back to under $10 again and you would have lost 90% of your investment!

3.11 Revenue Per Share

I like this statistic because it gives me an idea of how much earning power each share of the company has. Now of course not all of the revenue that's generated per share of stock can be converted fully into the final earnings per share at the bottom line, but it gives you an idea of the earnings strength that each share of stock has.

Now if the company finds ways to become more efficient (companies are always looking for ways to improve efficiency) more of that per share revenue will show up at the bottom line and the price of the stock will rise accordingly. The revenue per share is also a measure of the real strength and marketing power of the company. Sometimes revenue is increasing sharply with time but earnings per share may lag because of inefficiencies or because of expenses caused by the quest to increase revenue. Time may show that earnings per share will also increase rapidly when the company adjusts to the higher revenue condition.

For example, if you are going to buy 100 shares of a company, would you rather buy a company's stock whose revenue is $0.50 per share, or a stock that delivers over $70 per share (like Exxon) if the prices of the two stocks were the same?

In the first case you may be buying a stock that is probably hyped up by excessive expectation of future revenue but is not yet really generating much revenue per share (or there is a ridiculously large number of shares that have been issued with each share of being of little value as a result), but in the second case you are buying a stock that already has a lot of revenue for each share of their stock, and is definitely a viable "going business".

Maybe the hyped- up stock will eventually generate a lot of revenue and surpass even $100 per share. But if you buy that stock, it is a very speculative type of investment that may not be really suitable to your investment objectives.

3.12 Quarterly Revenue Growth

This statistic tells you what the current state of the company's marketing efforts and/or the demand for their products is. If you see that the quarterly revenue growth is small, or even negative in some cases, this is an indication that growth of the company's business in the future is not likely, and it is a red flag that perhaps you should not buy this particular stock.

I like to see quarterly revenue growth of at least 10% for a growth company, but you will not usually expect this to be true of high-income stocks which we will discuss later. Other companies' revenue growth may be due to a cyclical demand.

For example, the oil industry is a cyclical industry because the price of oil will increase and decrease over long periods of time. Right now, Exxon's quarterly revenue growth rate is about 26% which is very good, but I suspect that this is mainly because the price of oil has been increasing at the time, I am writing this book.

3.13 Quarterly Earnings Growth

One of the most important statistics is the quarterly earnings growth. Here I emphasize "earnings" because this is a bottom-line kind of statistic, as opposed to quarterly revenue growth. For example, in the case of Exxon again, where the quarterly revenue growth was about 26%, the quarterly earnings growth increased to 69%! In addition to the great number for earnings growth for a large cap company, what else is interesting here?

It is interesting because it shows that currently Exxon is doing something great to improve their earnings at a higher rate than they could generate revenue. This is one of the hallmarks of a great company, that they can get great results by improving their efficiency. Now we don't know how they did it, but if they laid off workers to achieve it, that is business honey!

3.14 Net Income Available to Common Stock

This is a good statistic to look at because it shows you how much money the company earns that *could be* applied to the common stock. In most cases, not all of the money the company earns will be applied to their company stock. A lot of this money will be used for investing in capital equipment, acquisitions, investments, buying back company stock, or a host of other uses.

If it is a significant amount, and it is invested in tangible assets, it may increase the book value of the company which may in turn have some positive effect on the price of the company stock.

There is one type of stock where most of this money is actually paid to stockholders as dividends. This type of company is called a REIT or Real Estate Investment Trust. These companies are regulated by the government and are required to pay at least 90% of their earnings out to stockholders each year.

Some of these stocks are high income stocks as a result of the 90% requirement. I like to buy these stocks if interest rates a generally declining because the stock value will generally increase as people seek to find better dividends in the market place.

On the other hand, I do not buy income stocks if I know that the Federal Reserve plans to raise interest rates, because the price of the stock will usually decline as interest rates rise.

This is also true of utility stocks and other stocks that are mainly bought for their dividends.

3.15 Earnings per Share or Diluted Earnings per Share

The earnings per share statistic, properly diluted as necessary, is a bottom-line statistic that is probably the most important statistic for a company, but by itself it is not sufficient to make a decision to buy a stock. Maybe it is only a temporary amount for the last year and that the next year might be zero or even a negative value.

What we should look at is whether or not the earnings are consistent from year-to-year, and hopefully even increasing from year-to-year. Once you know what the earnings per share are and the price of the stock is currently, then you can easily compute the P/E (price-to-earnings ratio) by dividing the current price by the earnings per share to obtain the most accurate P/E at the current time.

You will see that in general, the higher the earnings per share that a company has, the higher the price of the stock is. This is because the more capital gain or income an investment returns, the higher its value is. The principle is also true in a type of real estate that is called "income property". In real estate a knowledgeable investor will look for properties that are not priced higher than 10 times the income the property returns, depending on the prevailing interest rates.

A similar rule prevails in the stock market that a stock is properly priced if the price is not greater than 10 times the earnings per share. Of course, we know that some "hot" or high growth stocks are priced higher than their current earnings per share, but this is because expectations are that these certain stocks will have rapidly increasing earnings per share as time progresses and are therefore worth more currently.

As I am writing this book, Exxon stock closed at a price of $85.22 and the reported diluted earnings per share is $7.02. So, dividing 7.02 into 85.22 we arrive at a figure of 12.14 for the approximate price-to-earnings ratio for the day. Now this calculation is only as accurate as the value that is reported as the diluted earnings per share statistic that was reported.

We have to keep in mind that the real earnings per share from day-to-day cannot really be known, and it can also be drastically dropping without our knowledge, or it could be rapidly increasing and we would not know that either. We will have to wait for the next earnings report that comes out.

The earnings report will usually be available quarterly but sometimes up-dated information is made available through news releases from the company or information that is in the news. This is another reason why you need to follow the news on the company you are planning to invest in, or that you have already invested in.

3.16 Total Cash

The total cash statistic is interesting and you should know how much cash a company has on hand. Generally, the more cash a company has on hand, the stronger it is. But the number should be compared to the company's total debt. If a company has $1B in total cash but it owes $100B, the $1B in cash is not very significant. Exxon has $12.8B in total cash, but it owes $15.9B, so its total cash could be better or its debt could be lower and the stock would look better.

A large amount of cash available to a company gives it the advantages of more money available for R & D, developing new products, spending more on marketing, acquiring other businesses, and expanding into new plants, equipment, and developing new markets. In that sense cash is king in terms of the company's strength and potential when used efficiently and intelligently.

3.17 Total Cash per Share

The total cash per share is a meaningful statistic that you can use to compare the stock's share liquid cash value to other companies. Note that this not the same as book value per share which takes into account not only the cash on hand but also all other tangible assets the companies. For example, at the time of writing this book, Exxon has $2.61 in cash per share which is not a really spectacular number mainly because of the massive total number of shares the company has outstanding of 4.93B. See 'Shares Outstanding' described below.

3.18 Total Debt

Total debt is exactly what it means. It is the total amount of money the company owes to banks, bond holders, and all others that the company owes money to. But stock is not debt. The company never has to buy back its stock, although a company, from time-to-time may buy back some of its stock, or issue additional stock, if it looks advantageous to do so.

Ideally, we would like to own stock in companies that have no debt, and there are stocks like that, but that does not mean that you should buy, because there may be other statistics that are negative indicators that outweigh the no-debt condition. So, look at the total debt the company has and compare it to the total cash it has.

A reasonable amount of debt is ok if the company has enough cash to operate with and invest in new business opportunities, such as acquisitions, new oil wells, new apartments, or whatever their business investment interest is.

Large capital investments usually entail some kind of external financing to make them possible. For example, people usually get a mortgage to buy or build a house when they cannot easily pay all cash for the property. Another reason is that sometimes certain types of companies will borrow money at say 10%, and then by making intelligent investments they can earn 15% to 20% on investments such as real estate, and other activities. Even individuals may borrow money for a house though they could pay cash because they can obtain a mortgage at say 5%, which is approximately the rate as I write this, and they can invest their money instead in income stocks and earn 10% to 15% interest. By the way, some people buy a home for investment purposes, but most people buy a home to live in, and their home can be thought of as something that gives a family a measure of security over the years, especially after it is paid for, or it has accumulated a high percentage of equity over the amount of the mortgage.

Another thing to consider is that the value of money generally declines with time, and in periods when the value of money is declining rapidly (high inflation), it is not a bad idea to owe money especially if the interest rate is low and fixed. On the other hand, if cash is becoming more valuable, you will see the dollar value of non-liquid assets such as real estate, and commodities start to decline in value (a deflationary condition.) In this case it is not a good idea to be in debt and it is better to convert assets to cash before they decline further in dollar value.

This reminds me of a story about a widow who was rich before the depression started but lost all of her assets in the stock market crash of 1929. Fortunately, she had cash hidden behind a picture on her wall and she used that cash to survive the depression. The moral of this story is to always keep some cash where you can get it easily, and remember that banks can fail. Also, a safety deposit box can be raided by the authorities for any valuables you may have stored in the box.

Lately the Federal Deposit Insurance Corporation has had its liquidity questioned. Even the Federal Government can default on its obligations. This is a possibility as I am writing this book. Then, why should anyone put their money into Treasury bonds at very low interest rates, if the government might default on those bonds? Professional bond traders know how to trade this market profitably by using margin and other clever investment techniques.

Buying quality bonds is a valid investment technique if you buy for the long term. I do not recommend buying bonds on margin because you can lose your entire investment if the bond price turns against you.

Some bond funds have good returns with relatively good safety. Here are some examples:

Vanguard Long Term Corporate Bond ETF VCLT

+11% 52 weeks

Vanguard Intermediate Term Corporate Bond ETF VCIT
+7.5% 52 weeks

3.19 Total Debt to Equity Ratio

The total debt to equity ratio is the total liabilities of the company divided by the total stockholder's equity. It is also a measure of the aggressiveness of the company in financing their activities, or in other words how much they are leveraged.

In the case of Exxon, they have a debt-to-equity ratio of approximately 10. An example of a highly leverage position is one in which a man who buys an apartment house with a 20% down payment and an 80% first mortgage. But in order to finance the deal he obtains a second mortgage to cover the 20% down payment requirement. In this case, the leverage is virtually 100%, and he has no net equity in the property.

So, the debt-to-equity ratio is an infinite value and cannot even be calculated. If he simply paid all cash from his savings, his leverage would be 0%. I think the total debt to equity ratio should be less than 20, but this also depends on the type of company and its business. Companies that invest in real estate as their primary business usually have a high value of the total debt to equity ratio. An example of this kind of a company is Arlington Investment which invests mainly in real estate and has a debt-to-equity ratio of over 250.

3.20 Current Ratio or Quick Ratio

The current ratio or 'quick ratio' is computed by dividing current assets by current liabilities. A current asset is one that can be converted to cash within 12 months or within the current fiscal year. A current liability is one which will become due within 12 months or the current fiscal year.

Most companies try to keep extra money invested in assets that earn interest, expected capital gain, or income of some kind. So, a lot of companies will have a current ratio less than one, but usually not much less than one. An example is Exxon with a current ratio of 0.98. This is usually true of companies that have a high rate or turnover of their inventory and that accounts payable (on purchased inventory) are becoming due at a slower rate.

McDonalds is an example of this kind of business with a current ratio of 0.90. From the point of view of the company's supplier, and maybe some investors, it is better to have a current ratio of about 2.0 because the supplier is more confident that he will be paid and perhaps provide the company with more lenient credit terms on purchases.

A ratio that is much larger than 2.0 may indicate that the company has inefficient management or it is just not utilizing capital the way that it should. On the other hand, if a company has a current ratio of about 0.6 or 0.5 or less, it might be in financial trouble and investors should be very cautious about buying such stocks.

These kinds of stocks would be of more interest to short sellers who sell the stock without owning it (they have to borrow the shares from someone, usually the broker they deal with) hoping that the price will drop and that they will have a profit when they buy it back at a lower price than they sold it at. I don't recommend short selling because if you are wrong and the price of the stock goes up instead of down, the loss can be *unlimited* and it can be very difficult to liquidate the position.

3.21 Book Value per Share

This statistic should give you an idea of the minimum value of your stock in the event of a massive downturn in stock prices. Normally, the book value of a share should be the lowest price of a good stock you would ever see. But unfortunately, in panic situations, the price of a stock can even go below its book value.

In the case of Exxon, the book value is a little over $30 per share as I write this book. At its current price of a little over $84, the stock would have to drop over 64% to reach its book value. This large a drop is not very likely with a good quality stock like Exxon.

Most major stock market declines are in the 15% to 25% range with some extreme drops of up to 50%, and there are some extreme case where stocks have dropped even more than 50%. In 1929, the market started a series of declines that eventually caused it to drop approximately 90% of its value before the crash.

There are mutual funds that were started before 1929 and if you could have invested in them before 1929 and held them without selling until today, you would have a good increase in your assets, at least in today's dollars. So, the 'Buy and Hold' theory of stock investing may be a good way to invest even in today's market with instant computer trading and high volatility, if you have the patience to do so.

I have a friend who stuck with one stock for 30 years and as a result he is a wealthy person today even by American standards. My own personal belief is that you continue to hold stocks that perform in a reasonable fashion as long as there is not some disastrous news or statistics that indicate a serious loss may result if you continue to hold the stock. So, I hold stocks as long as I can, but I periodically check on their performance and statistics, and I will sell and replace stocks that look bad for one reason or another.

Once every six months or a year, you should look at the performance of each stock you own. Sell the stocks that have not performed, and use the proceeds to buy better stocks. If I have a stock that has more than doubled since I bought, I usually sell one half of it to regain my original investment and then just continue to hold the other half.

3.22 Operating Cash Flow

Operating Cash Flow (OCF) is defined as total revenues less operating expenses. In actuality there are some adjustments that are made so it is representative of net income per share. The details of the adjustments are beyond the scope of this book. But the figure is a good one that you can compare it to total revenue.

For example, in the case of Exxon, their OCF is $52.2 B compared to $363 B in revenue. Dividing OCF by total revenue we find that Exxon's OCF is over 14% of revenue. This is a very good value and shows that Exxon's operating efficiency is excellent. If the percentage was very small, e.g., less than 5% it would indicate that perhaps something is wrong.

There may be a large cash drain in operations somewhere, or maybe a subsidiary is losing a lot of money. This is not always information that is readily available and does not otherwise show up in the statistics, except that the net earnings per share will probably be low also.

Another way to look at it is, if I am only earning 5% on a business, I might as well close that business and just invest in stocks that pay a dividend of 5% or more. Then I could just go fishing.

3.23 Levered Free Cash Flow

Levered Free Cash Flow, sometimes referred to as just Free Cash Flow (we will call it FCF) is cash that is available after all expenses and it is not earmarked for anything else (like capital projects or planned investments, etc.)

FCF is available for distribution to stock and bond holders as dividends or cash distributions, or for emergency use. What I like about a large amount of FCF is that it gives the company options, in the case that some unexpected event should require emergency cash.

Or maybe a terrific investment opportunity comes along and there is "free" cash available to put to use whereas if there were little or no FCF, the company could not act on the opportunity. In other words, a company that has a lot of FCF has a lot of financial power, and investors like to see a lot of Free Cash Flow. Unfortunately, the FCF statistic is not always available.

3.24 Beta

Beta is a measure of the price volatility of the stock computed over a period of time. Regression analysis is used to compute its value for each stock. I won't get into the details of the computation. If the value of beta for a stock is 1.0 this means that the stock will have the same volatility as the stock market and the same amount of risk is indicated as if you bought a basket of stocks that closely represented the market. One such index would be the S & P 500.

If beta is higher than 1.0, such as a value of 1.2, this would indicate that the stock is 20% more volatile than the market, and also has of risk that is 20% higher than the market. On the other hand, if a stock's beta is less than 1.0, such as Exxon's beta of 0.44 currently, it is less volatile than the stock market and also has an indicated risk that is lower as well.

Of course, you cannot go only by the value of beta in assessing a stock's risk because there are a lot of other factors to consider as well. Usually, utility stocks have lower beta values than for example high technology stocks. Apple stock has a beta of 1.11 so the volatility of Apple is 11% higher than the market.

Another thing to remember is that the profit potential is higher with a stock that has a higher beta because there could be a large upside move in a short time, whereas a low beta stock is unlikely to move very fast. Of course, the higher the beta, the stock could also make a large downside move and if you have bought the stock to hold, you will be subject to that risk.

Companies that have a very large amount of high value shares held by institutions and the public, are likely to have a relatively low beta value because even with a large volume of shares traded each day, it is still only a small effect on stock price because of the large number of shares outstanding.

3.25, 52 Week Change

The 52-week change is important to check and compare to the 52 week change for some market index such as the S & P500 52 week change (see below), or other stocks that are in similar industries. It is also good to compare this number to the 52 week low price value (see below.) Why is the 52 week change number important? Well for one thing, if the S & P was up 17% for the 52 prior weeks, would you be interested in a stock that had only achieved a 5% or 10% increase during the same period? Not unless, you knew something that made you think the stock was about to make a major upward move for some known factual reason.

I would not buy such a stock on just a rumor of a price run-up or even some technical chart price moves which might work out or might not work out. (No matter how good a stock's chart looks at first glance, or even after extensive analysis, it is not enough for a buy decision without other factual data to go on.)

In the case of Exxon, the 52-week high was 33% vs. 17% for the S & P500, or almost double the index change. Conclusion? Exxon definitely beat the S & P500 for the 52-week period and this was a great performance.

Did you know that there are very few mutual funds that beat the S & P500 index on a regular basis? Now, I should mention that the period I am talking about is also a period when oil prices were climbing rapidly, so there were special commodity market circumstances that are probably a big factor in Exxon's rise. So, you should compare the 52 weeks change for Exxon to that of other oil industry stocks before you conclude that Exxon is a great stock.

3.26 S & P 500 52 Week Change

This statistic is the percentage change in the Standard and Poor's 500 Stock Index over the last 52 weeks as listed in currently available statistics. This index includes 500 stocks chosen from a broad cross-section of stocks of different industries.

The stocks are vetted in the sense that they have to meet certain fundamental requirements that the index uses to select what they think are the best 500 stocks available. If a stock that has been included in the index, starts slipping so that it no longer meets the index's criteria, it will be deleted from the list. This is a statistic you can use to compare stocks you are researching.

As I explained above, you will generally look for stocks that consistently outperform the S & P500 except in special situations which we will discuss later. Another thing that this statistic tells you is whether the general market of "good" stocks has or is in a "bull" or "bear market".

A "bull market" is a market that is or has been moving to the up-side and usually it is generally expected to continue moving up by most investors. Of course, this can be a "self-fulfilling prophecy" if investors expect the market to go up and keep on buying stock.

A "bear market" differs from the "bull market" in that the direction of movement is negative instead of positive. Otherwise, the same principle of the "self-fulfilling prophecy" still applies as investors sell stocks because they expect stocks to go down in value.

Bull and bear markets are also usually the result of some economic conditions that investors perceive as "good" or "bad" for business and will likely cause stocks to go up or down in value. By the way, you can consider each stock to be an individual market that could be in either a bull or bear market phase of its stock price history. Again, you can quickly tell this by comparing its 52 weeks change against the S & P500 52 week change and determine if its price history indicates that it is in its own bear or bull market.

Another way is to find a chart on the stock and look at the one-year price performance. We will discuss charts later. By the way most companies go through at least two phases of price history. Early at the start of a company its price may go up rapidly as it gains strength and market share (not all stocks do.)

There may be many stock splits and people who invested in the stock and continued to hold it might become wealthy if they had a big enough investment to start with. Eventually, the company will mature and stop splitting their stock. It may go for many years in this stable condition.

Unless the company is providing good dividends and even increasing its dividends each year, there is really no reason to hold the stock anymore as you will have neither capital gain nor income from it. Eventually it may move into a third phase which is decline and possibly even bankruptcy or closure of the business.

Some examples of companies that started out good and then declined are Woolworth's, A & P, Packard, Studebaker, and many more. Sometimes a company will recover and start a new cycle of increasing stock values. Current examples are General Motors that has come out of bankruptcy, and Microsoft which has moved into a new bull phase with some new technology called "cloud computing."

If you research a lot of stocks you will see some of these stocks. A very good company will still be in a phase of multi-year increasing strength and performance. Examples of these kinds of companies are Apple Computer, IBM, Oracle, and others. Some examples of relatively stagnant companies in the mature phase are Johnson & Johnson, Pfizer, and a lot of other so-called "Large Cap" companies.

3.27 52 Week High

The 52-week high for a stock tells you what the maximum price is or has been in the last 52 weeks before the statistic is currently reported. You should compare the present market price of the stock to the 52-week high and ask yourself these questions: Is the stock now at its peak (very close to or at the

52-week high), and if it is, will it now take a dive to lower levels?

As I write this, Exxon closed at a price of $77 per share. Its 52-week high is about $88, so I would think that Exxon is not at a peak, and it might be a candidate for investment, if other factors and statistics are acceptable. I never feel comfortable about buying a stock at a peak value. There would have to be a very important reason to do so.

I would rather buy a stock when it is close to its projected low, as I call it. You can easily determine what a 'projected low' is for most stocks by printing the chart of a stock that covers at least 6 months, or better for a year, and then, using a ruler, draw a straight line through the low points in the price of the stock over the period shown on the chart. You will see the low points easily.

On some computerized stock analysis sites, you can do this on the computer screen, or copy and paste the chart into "Paint", or some other drawing program, or just print the chart, and then draw a straight line on the chart image.

For most stocks that show a generally positive trend, you will find that the low points will fall on a straight line that you have drawn. Then just project this line to see where the next low is likely to be, or if it is at a low now then you might consider buying it.

On the other hand, if the price is currently higher than your line and closer to a peak in the price history you might wait until it is closer to a low point as predicted by the line you drew on your chart. Drawing this line is about the most complicated thing that I do in the area of "technical analysis."

There are a lot of other techniques or ways to do technical analysis, but this is beyond the scope of the present book. Of course, there is no guarantee that just because the stock price lows fall on your line, that it will continue to do this in the future.

One more thing about this line is if the last dip on the chart dips below your line established by the previous lows on the chart, this is a signal that the stock may be on a track to establish a new low, and you should not buy it until it shows a better trend.

By the way, if your trend line shows a continually dropping set of lows, it is most likely not a good stock to consider any further for a 'long' position. By using the term 'long' we are talking about an ownership position where you have either acquired the stock by buying it outright, or by some other method, and it is likely that you will hold it for some period of time.

If I said I am 'short' in the stock, I mean that I have sold the stock without actually owning the stock in the first place, hoping to replace it later by buying it at a lower price than I sold it at, for a nice profit. In order to do this, you have to borrow the stock temporarily from someone, usually the stock broker or his company. You will have to have a certain amount of value in your account to get the broker's approval to do this 'short' transaction, and your account would have to be set up so you have prior approval to do this type of transaction.

By the way, I don't recommend that you short stock unless you are a well-heeled professional investor. If you short a stock and the price keeps going up instead of down, your losses can be unlimited, or in other words your assets could be wiped out. Always be aware of what the risk of an investment is to you on any transaction you do.

3.28, 52 Week Low
The 52-week low is important because it gives you a quick idea of what the lowest value of the stock could be in the next 52 weeks. It also tells you how well the stock has done after that low by comparing it to the present stock price. If the current price of the stock is close to the 52-week low, it's an indication that the stock is not doing well, or it is even going lower perhaps.

Look at the chart you might have made that I described above in the section titled "52 Week High". Is the 52-week low one of the points that fit on your straight line or is it an anomalous point that was an exceptional drop was very temporary?

It would be acceptable to ignore one low point on your chart as long as it is not very recent and you can relate it too some unusual circumstance such as a large market drop that happened at the same time. In the case of Exxon, the 52-week low is much lower than the current value and is not very significant at this time. But in the case of Exxon, you will have trouble drawing a straight line through the full year.

Why? Because the chart shows that you would need to draw two lines as the chart trend changed recently forming a down trend line for the lows. This change was most likely due to the recent drop in oil prices which would also most likely result in lower profit levels and a decline in the price of the stock.

The price of oil is usually cyclical but now there is a new factor in oil prices, whereas the output of USA and Canada has been increasing due to shale oil production. So, if you were going to invest in Exxon you might take a very long-range view with the theory that over a long period of time oil prices should increase because of declining reserves (which may not be true anymore.)

Also, this theory could be incorrect if demand also drops due to some technical breakthrough, for example, a light weight high energy battery is developed to make electric cars cheap and massed produced.

Now we have better technology in battery manufacturing with Lithium batteries, and possibly even better batteries coming. If electric vehicles suddenly become cheap and widely produced, the demand for oil would probably drop precipitously. How soon will that happen? It is looking more likely every year.

3.29 50 Day Moving Average

The 50 Day Moving Average is an important statistic when you are checking the performance of a stock on its price vs. time chart. The 50 Day Moving Average is defined simply as the average stock price for the last 50 days that is up-dated every day.

Every day the previous 50-day average is up-dated with the average price on the next closing day by weighting the next day closing price at $1/50^{th}$ relative to the previous 50 days. What is important about the 50-day moving average? First of all, if a stock dips below its 50-day moving average, it may signal a change in the general trend of the stock from positive to negative.

Conversely, if a stock goes above its 50-day moving average, it may signal a trend change from negative to positive. This is a simple rule of thumb, but keep in mind that a stock can also change back and forth across its 50-day moving average line from one day to the next, or one week to the next, so it is not necessarily a definitive measure of the longer-term movement of the stock.

For example, over the next month or year. I like to see a stock stay well above its 50-day moving average which indicates that the stock has high momentum. But what if a stock starts to drop below its 50-day moving average? Is there a lower value of the moving average to consider? To have a better rule of thumb to go by, you also need to look at the 200 Day Moving Average, which we discuss next.

3.30 200 Day Moving Average

The 200-day moving average is important because it shows you what the longer-term trend of the stock price is, and it is also the statistic you should watch when buying a stock or considering selling an underperforming stock. The 200-day moving average is computed in the same way as the 50-day moving average except that the data included in each calculation goes back to include the last 200 days.

If the stock moves below both its 50-day moving average and its 200-day moving average, this is an indication that a bear market is probable for the stock in the immediate future. So, what should you look for on the price chart for the stock? I like to see a stock moving well above both its 50-day moving average and its 200-day moving average.

If it is running above both the 50 day and the 200 day, this indicates that it is a healthy stock price movement and possibly the stock is moving into a bull market phase of its growth, or it is already a bull market of its own. One thing to note is if the overall stock market is in a period of instability such as a large downward move, you may see a lot of good stocks go below their 200-day moving average during such a time.

But a good high- quality stock which has financial strength and good prospects for the future will very likely recover quickly once the market stabilizes. On the other hand, a low-quality stock which is weak financially and has marketing and profit problems may not recover from the downtrend. Its price may never be back up again where it was and if you owned such a stock you would have what I call a "loser stock" that would make a good candidate to sell and put the proceeds into a better stock or other investment.

If I think the stock market is shaky and headed for a major drop that may have a significant effect on my assets, I may use "stop-loss" orders set to initiate an active sell order if the stock price drops below a certain percentage of my purchase price. The sell point might be 7% to 10% depending on how tightly I want to control my asset values. Professionals usually insist on selling any stock that drops below 7%, but I have found that this can result in a pre-mature sell order and losing a position that later on may turn out to be a profitable position.

I think how tightly you set your stop loss point depends on how much confidence you have in the quality of the stocks you own. If I know I own a great stock that has great long-term prospects, I don't think I would be very happy if I was sold out of it on a temporary market downturn.

3.31 Average Volume

If you plan to buy a stock you need to have an idea of how much share trading your stock has. Why? For a number of reasons: First of all, if the trading volume on the stock is very small, for example less than 10,000 shares a day, you may have some trouble buying or selling the stock.

Wait times may be long and by the time your order comes to the trading floor, the price may have already changed and your order is no longer executable. If you really want to buy it you will have to put in a new order at a higher price. Or your order was so slow going through that the stock price dropped substantially while your order was waiting to be placed. But you can be sure that in this case, your order will be executed at the higher price you specified in your buy at a limit order. (Never place a "market price" price order.)

You could be charged anything on a market order, especially on low volume stocks. (A limit order is an order to buy or sell either not over a certain price, the limit price, or under the limit price in case of a sell order. A market order is an instruction to sell the stock at the prevailing market price, but note that the floor trader decides what the market price is and in theory he could charge anything that he wanted to.)

Another reason is that there could be a large spread between the "bid" and "asked prices". For example, if you are trying to sell 1000 shares, the bid price might be $20 and the asked price might be $25 or even $30, when you thought you could sell the shares at the listed price or something in between, say $24. Now you find out that you can only get $20. (The "bid" price is the price the floor trader is willing to pay for shares you want to sell, and "asked" price is the price at which that the trader is willing to sell you shares.)

Or the price will suddenly drop on the stock just because you are trying to place a large order of say 1000 shares (when the average daily volume is only 5000 shares.) On the other hand, low trading volume can work to your advantage when you are building a position in a stock. At one time I bought shares in an obscure low volume stock that was a low-price stock.

Every time I bought a reasonably large number of shares, the price of the stock would immediately increase after I had placed my order because my order was significant relative to the average daily trading volume. As I continued to place orders over a period of time, the stock would keep increasing in price and it would not drop back down again to its former price.

Eventually I had a very profitable position in the stock. Usually, the average investor will have an easier time if he invests primarily in the larger well- known companies that have large trading volume, for example at least 100,000 shares a day or more, because his trades will be executed faster, and he is less likely to get ripped off on a trade because of slow trading or a large bid to asked spread.

Another factor in stock trading involving trading volume is at periods of time when the price of the stock is making a significant move in price, either up or down. If the volume is high on an upswing, this means that there is sudden increasing interest in the stock and the stock has what professional traders call "momentum".

On the other hand, if there is a lot of volume on a price down swing it may mean that something important is happening and there is a rush to dump it by a large number of investors. Finally, if the price of the stock is going up but the volume is weak and fading, the price rise is not likely to be sustained and the stock may start to fall.

On a rally we want the volume to increase as the price rises or at least the volume is good and is sustained so we have confidence that we have a true rally and not just a short interlude before the price goes back down to where it was or even lower. This kind of analysis is vital to short term or day traders that want to make a profit on their buy and sell strategies. (I don't recommend short term trading for persons just getting started in stock market investing.)

3.32 Shares Outstanding

The total Shares Outstanding is the total number of shares owned by the public plus the restricted shares owned by insiders and officers of the company. It does not include shares that the company has repurchased. You can divide the total earnings of the company by the shares outstanding to obtain an approximate value of the earnings per share for the company.

You can use the shares outstanding number to calculate a lot of other statistics that you might be interested in, such as revenue per share, free cash per share, total sales per share, etc. It is good to always compare stocks on the basis of the statistics per share as a way to normalize your data.

3.33 Share Float

The 'float' is the total number of shares that the public owns and that are available for trading by the public. For large companies, the float is usually almost the same as the total shares outstanding, but this is not always the case, especially when an individual owns more that 50% of the shares.

You need to be aware of this because, if one stockholder owns a lot or most of the shares outstanding, he might suddenly sell a large block of shares on the market and depress the stock price significantly. So always compare the 'float' against the 'total shares outstanding' and calculate the difference.

If you are fortunate to have a lot of money to invest, be sure to look at the float. You may have enough money to gain control of a company that you like. This is how Warren Buffet got started building his fortune. He took control of a small textile company and then eventually built his financial empire in insurance companies using the textile company as a base of operations.

3.34 Percentage Held by Institutions

The percentage of the float held by institutions is important for you to know because the more that is owned by institutions, the more confident you can be that the stock is a good stock to own. For example, the Exxon float is more than 49% owned by institutions. We already know that Exxon is a good stock, even though it can be drastically affected by ups and downs in the oil commodity prices.

The fact that almost 50% of the float is owned by institutions is a pretty good indication that the professional investors working for the institutions also think that Exxon is a good stock to own over the long haul.

3.35 Shares Short or Short Interest

Shares Short are the total shares that have been sold short from the float. Short shares are shares that people have sold without actually owning the shares. They have borrowed the shares from someone, usually their broker, and they will have to buy the shares back at some time to 'cover' their short position.

If their short position has a large negative profit, they may get a call from their broker ordering the short seller to either buy the shares to cover their position, or put up additional capital to cover the negative position. If their position is in a positive profit range, the short seller can maintain his or her position indefinitely unless he has an agreement or limitation on their account with the broker (or whoever he borrowed the stock from) to cover his position within a certain time period.

If the short seller is well-heeled and has plenty of capital in his or her account, the broker will probably not bother the short seller. Selling stock short is one of the trading techniques that can cause the trader to have unlimited losses that possibly wipe out the trader's assets if he is not careful. Professional traders usually don't have a problem and watch their positions carefully, trading out of them when the positions start looking bad, or are showing significant losses that are not likely to improve. I don't recommend short selling for the average trader, or someone just starting out as an investor in the stock market.

3.36 Short Ratio

The short ratio is the total number of shares sold short divided by the average daily trading volume. Another way to say it is that the short ratio is the number of days that would be required to cover all short sales at the average daily trading volume for the stock.

A high short ratio indicates that a lot of people think that the stock is likely to drop in value and so they have sold the shares short. For example, in the case of Exxon the short ratio is 1.6 at the time I am writing this, whereas the short ratio for Oracle, a high technology stock, is 0.80, one-half of the value for Exxon.

The higher ratio for Exxon probably reflects the current decline in the oil commodity prices, and so traders expect the price of Exxon stock to decline over the short term. As a trader you need to look at the short ratio carefully and compare it to other stocks that you know to be good stocks and relatively stable in price.

When you look at the short ratio statistic, realize that this number reflects the cumulative wisdom of traders on which way the stock is likely to move in the near future. If the short ratio is less than 1.0 you can be fairly certain that traders do not expect the stock price to decline significantly in the near-term.

On the other hand, if the short ratio is greater than about 5.0, I would be very careful before I established a significant long position in the stock. It is OK, however, if you make periodic small purchases at a fixed dollar amount over a long period of time. This technique is called 'dollar-cost-averaging' which we will explain later.

3.37 Short Covering

Sometimes if the market is increasing rapidly and most stocks are increasing at the time, a situation may develop that is called a "short squeeze" when a lot of traders that have sold stocks short are forced to buy the shares on the open market to cover their short sales and avoid very large losses. This process is called "short covering".

The importance of the short squeeze to an investor that is considering buying stocks, is that it may be an opportunity to pick up good stocks that have high short ratios because they are likely to show a good increase in price due to the short squeeze that is occurring. The investor is in effect taking a "contrarian" position when he buys a stock against the prevailing opinion of investors.

3.38 Program Trading

This is not a statistic but it is a good time to talk about this trading method and its effects on the market. You should learn to love the new "program trading" methods using computers that are popular currently because it is here to stay.

Usually, program trading tends to stabilize the market during periods of decline (and also if the market is increasing in prices.) Why? Because if stock prices decline low enough, the programs will automatically start buying certain stocks that are being automatically traded by the professionals (you have to be very knowledgeable to set up and do this kind of trading.)

Of course, if the prices rise to a certain point, the programs will automatically start selling certain stocks which can lead to a sharp downturn. Sometimes we see unreasonable sharp drops in some stock that has been triggered by something and causes the program trading to initiate a large sell order.

Program trading, *if it is working properly*, will tend to level out the market. But if the total population of program traders, execute a large volume of trades at the same time, the net effect can be that the market becomes unstable and fluctuates wildly. It is like a large bell that is hit with its gong, and keeps ringing for a long time because there is little or no damping in the system.

We are seeing this effect in the market gyrations of August 2011. Unfortunately, there is no way to force traders to build a little 'damping' into their programs to stop the wild fluctuations.

3.39 Insider Trading

Insider trading is available information that you can find on individual companies. This information is important when you are analyzing a stock. If insiders are buying stock in the company they are associated with (officers, board members, etc.), you know that insiders think that their stock will increase and this may be just the information you are looking for to clinch your buy decision. Or, if insiders are selling, this may be justification for selling the stock if there are other negative factors as well.

Sometimes insiders will sell stock just because the stock is at a high. This is not necessarily a problem except that you should realize that maybe the price of the stock is too high and the insiders are selling while the selling is good because they expect it to go lower in the near future.

3.40 Gold

Gold is not a statistic. It is a commodity. But you can use the price moves to gauge the anxiety of investors. If the price of gold is rising rapidly, this is an indication that investors are nervous and are moving from stock equities and other risk type investments into gold.

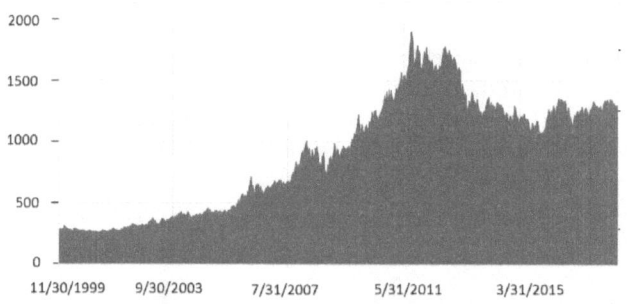

Fig. 2, The Historical Price of Gold in USD.

The price of gold has had its ups and downs but gold has maintained a certain intrinsic value over centuries. The fact that gold has increased in price is a reflection of the declining value of the dollar rather than a change intrinsic value of gold. The demand for gold has remained relatively constant as has the supply.

So, when supply and demand are relatively constant the intrinsic value can be considered to be more or less constant. The price (as opposed to the intrinsic value) is primarily determined by the value of the US dollar which has consistently dropped over the years.

That is not to say the buying gold is without risk! Gold can go into a bear market just like any other commodity or equity stock. If you buy a lot of gold and the economy suddenly deflates like it did in the 1930's, your gold will become very cheap and possibly hard to convert to cash or some other currency, and cash will be king in this case.

If we go into an inflationary economy, the price of gold will rise it is true, but so will equities. So why buy any gold for investment? The experts say you should have from 10% to 15% of your assets in precious metals such as gold, silver, platinum, etc. But this is an opinion and should not be implemented unless you have very good reasons to do so. Examine the price charts and be sure you are not buying into a bear market!

Two major gold ETFs are IAU and GLD. Both have a B-risk rating. The ETFs are convenient as you do not have to personally store gold somewhere and pay storage fees, or store it at home which also presents difficulties.
People say that gold is a rare commodity. But gold is mined all over the world all the time. A lot of gold is held in jewelry, teeth, etc. It is used in electronic equipment such as computers, connectors, etc. A lot of it is recovered from junk that companies routinely process to remove precious and common metals, every day.

But suppose things get really bad. Like what? Maybe due to some natural or man-made disaster, the power grid goes down, then the computer and telecommunications networks.

The banks, the brokers, and the markets close down because they can't do business. You can't get cash out of the bank. You can't get into your safety deposit box. You better have some cash or something valuable to trade with at your home or somewhere you can get to it.

Maybe if you had converted your assets into gold such as bullion coins, and you had the coins available to you. Then if you need to go to the store to get groceries, and you don't have any cash, is the grocer going to be willing to accept your gold coins? Maybe a small grocer will, but he probably won't give you more than $100 for a coin that is worth $1000 or more.

I have described a far-out unlikely example, but I am illustrating the problem of trying to sell gold or trade gold for goods. I think cash is easier to use and most likely everyone would accept it even under the extreme conditions I described above.

Another place you can put your money that is in an inflationary period is in Treasury Inflation Protected Securities (TIPS.) TIPS are guaranteed by the US government. So, if you believe in the financial viability of the US government, this is an alternative.

3.41 Forward Annual Dividend Rate

As an income investor, this is the most important statistic on a company for me. This is the total of dividends the company is expected to pay in the coming year. Note the word 'expected'. Dividends are not guaranteed except on some kinds of bonds, like Treasury bonds or high- grade coupon bonds.

Companies may change their dividends at any time, increasing them, decreasing them, or even eliminating dividends in any given year. So, you must track each company you own stock in to make sure they are paying the dividends you expect. I like stocks that pay dividends in cash directly to my account, preferably on a monthly basis. Most companies pay their dividends quarterly.

Now if I find a company that pays a really high dividend, should I put all of my assets into that stock? No because, the stock may be very risky, and even if I could not find anything else wrong with the company, it is still not a good idea to put all of your assets into one stock.

My rule of thumb is to keep each investment I have in my portfolio at less than 10% of my total assets. Another thing to consider is that the higher the dividend a company pays, the more risk the investment most likely has for some reason. For example, an oil tanker company may pay a high dividend, but their business is very risky because there is a risk that an expensive tanker with an expensive load of oil could be damaged or even sunk.

Of course, the company will probably have some kind of disaster insurance, but people including even the owners or major stockholders will want a high return on their risky investments. So, the company pays a high dividend.

Actually, I like these kinds of stocks but again I limit my investments to 10% or less of assets. Diversification of your portfolio is still important even if you are only interested in income.

By the way, when a company pays a good dividend, the stock has a sort of a price "floor" because if the stock drops very low in price, the yield of the stock becomes large. If the company is sound with good fundamentals, people will start buying the stock and the stock will go back up in price. So, in the event of market downturns, I prefer to own stocks that pay good dividends as opposed to stocks that pay no dividends.

That is not to say that there is any guarantee against a substantial drop in price however, so you always need to be very careful in your stock selections that they have good fundamental statistics and watch the news on your stocks for any negative developments.

Of course, there is always the possibility that even though you have picked a good stock with good fundamentals and the news looks good, that your stock can suffer a sudden severe drop in price due to some unforeseen circumstance. This is another reason why stock professionals diversify their portfolios and don't invest in just one stock or a just a very few stocks. So, don't put all your eggs in one basket!

3.42 Trailing Annual Dividend Yield

The trailing annual dividend yield is not a critical statistic but it is an interesting one because it tells you one of three things. Either the yield has been increased from last year, it is the same, or it has been reduced compared to the forward annual dividend yield. It is desirable that the dividend has been increased, but sometimes economic circumstances will cause the company to decrease their dividend, or the economic circumstances have not allowed better results so the dividend stays the same.

Hopefully, the dividend has not been decreased because of poor investment results due to bad management. This possibility highlights the need to know as much as you can about the leaders of the company you are investing in, the company's business model, or external circumstances that are affecting performance.

Is the management team experienced? Do they have a good investment track record? Are they reputable people with integrity? Read the reports the company puts out, especially the annual report. Does the CEO have a good forward-looking message or is he just giving excuses for poor performance last year?

What new programs do they talk about? Are there any new developments? What is the management outlook on the prospects of the company for the future? What is the business model and is it appropriate? What external factors such as the economy and the market for the company's products have on company performance now and in the future?

3.43 Five Year Average Dividend Yield

The Five-Year Average Dividend Yield is another non-critical statistic, but again it is a good one to look at because it tells you what the long-term dividend is likely to be, at least over the next five years, if economic conditions are reasonably similar to the previous five years.

In looking at this statistic however, you must consider what the economic conditions have been over the last five years and what you think they are likely to be in the next five years. In order to make any reasonable prediction about the economy and the stock market over the next five years you will need to do some study in the area of economics and know something about economic indicators. We will talk about economic indicators later in this book.

3.44 Payout Ratio

Now the Payout Ratio is a very important statistic for the high-income stock investor. The payout ratio tells the amount of dividend that is being paid to shareholders relative to the earnings per share that the company has. If the payout ratio is small, this is a good thing because there is plenty of room to increase the dividend in the future without exceeding the earnings per share.

If a company is paying out a dividend that is higher than their current earnings per share, then there had better be a high rate of earnings growth rate or some other good reason for the high payout ratio. Otherwise, it is likely that the company cannot sustain their level of dividend payout and they will have to decrease the dividend payout at some time.

If the payout ratio is close to 1.0, I would consider it to be reasonable, but if it is higher than say 1.1, or 10% above the earnings per share, I would start to question whether or not the dividend is likely to be sustained or not. Take a look at the earnings growth rate. Is it 10%, 20%, or even higher, or is it stable? This is one of the main things to consider when judging whether or not the dividend payout is likely to be sustained or not.

3.45 Dividend Date

The dividend date is the day that the next dividend will be paid. Dividends are usually paid either monthly or quarterly. All other things being equal, I would rather get a dividend each month, as I can reinvest the money to earn more dividends as a way to get the equivalent of compound interest on a monthly basis.

3.46 Ex-dividend Date

The Ex-dividend Date is important to you when you are acquiring shares of the stock. You should buy the shares before the Ex-dividend date in order to capture the closest next dividend payout.

If you buy the shares just after the Ex-dividend Date, you will have to wait until the next payout date to get a dividend. This is not necessarily bad however, especially if you are buying the shares on a dip in price, or at a bargain price and you expect the price to rise significantly. If the dividends are paid monthly, you don't have long to wait long anyway.

3.47 Last Split Factor

The Last Split Factor tells what the last stock split was (if any), new shares per old shares. For example, a two for one split means that if you had 100 shares of a stock before the split, you would have 200 shares after the split. Note that the stock price is automatically adjusted immediately after a split. If your 100 shares were priced at $50 per share before the split, the shares will be priced at $25 per share after the split. The good thing about a stock split is that it allows small retail investors to buy the stock even if the company is growing fast and the stock price is rising fast accordingly.

Unfortunately, stock splits now seem to be out of favor. Some high technology stocks such as Amazon, Google, and others have reached prices over $1000 per share, and many more with prices over $100 per share. They do not seem to want to split their stocks. High price stocks make it difficult for the small retail investor to obtain reasonable quantities of shares of say 100 shares or higher. I like to buy at least 100 shares of a company's stock so that I have at least a 100 times multiplier on any dollar gains that the stock makes!

Stock splits are sometimes used by companies when they are young and in a growth phase to keep the price per share at a reasonable level for the retail investor. It is also known by the major owners of a young growing company that if they split the stock fairly frequently during its growth phase, the owners stand to gain substantially as the number of their shares increases with the splits and the price of each share also continues to increase.

In the recent past many people became millionaires by getting into the young growth stocks and holding such stocks for the long term. If you are a young person and willing to invest for the long term, you might consider looking for these kinds of stocks to invest in, even if the company is not splitting their stock.

As a company becomes mature and growth slows to a more sedate pace, the company usually stops splitting the stock, or the splits become much less frequent and un-predictable by outsiders as to when they will happen. Splits are usually two for one, but they could be (rarely) three to one, or some oddball split such as one and one-half to one.

Be aware that sometimes a company will do a reverse split if they feel that the price of their stock has fallen too low. For example, if a stock is selling for $1.50 per share, the company might do a one for ten split. In other words, if you owned 100 shares at $1.50 you now own only 10 shares at $15 shares.

You now have what is known as an odd-lot position in the stock and your stock could be a little harder to sell and probably sell at a premium below market price. If you were one of the insiders and owned 10,000,000 shares, a one for ten split would not be so bad because you would still own 1,000,000 shares at $15 per share.

Most institutional and professional investors will not buy stocks under $10 per share for this reason and other reasons.

So, think twice if you are investing in stocks that are priced under $10 per share. Now I don't want to discourage investors that speculate in penny stocks. Penny stocks can be very rewarding if you know how to pick the right ones.

3.48 The Last Split Date

The Last Split Date is a statistic that is usually not very important to the long- term investor, but it is to those who are looking for stocks that are in a growth phase and are frequently splitting their shares. Along with the last split date, the growth investor should look at a stock's historical chart that shows when recent stock splits have occurred.

Usually there is a sort of periodicity to the stock splits, for example once a year, or even six-month intervals. But there is also the stock price as an important influence on whether or not a stock is split. If the price of a stock is rising rapidly, stock splits tend to occur more frequently. Or if the stock price is rising steadily but not so rapidly, stock splits will usually not be so frequent.

An investor who is looking to make a lot of money should look for young fast growth stocks that have a recent history of frequent stock splits, if he or she can find any (stock splitting is currently out of favor for growth companies.) The investor should know however that it is inherently risky to put substantial funds into only one or a very few stocks as we have mentioned above.

There does seem to be a law in investing that the higher the reward, the higher the risk. This law is evident in stock trading, options trading, and many other types of investments. As a high- income stock investor, I take very high risks in order to earn the highest average dividend return that I can obtain from the market place.

For example, usually the higher the dividend rate is for a stock that invests in high income bonds, the more volatile the price of the stock tends to be. Some of the risk in high income stock investing can be handled by a high degree of diversification and investing for the long term.

For example, if you were a high- income investor you might be diversified over many different industries such as corporate bonds, industrial stocks, energy stocks, transportation stocks, telecommunications, real estate, finance, etc. I personally like the REIT (Real Estate Investment Trust.) These stocks have to pay out at least 90% of their earnings as dividends according to law.

4.0 Chapter 4 Economic Indicators

For the investor who is a trader as opposed to a long- term investor, he or she should be aware of certain economic indicators that can signal stock market moves or economic downturns to a certain extent. As with a lot of other things, so-called economic indicators are not infallible at predicting future market or economic conditions.

However, I have identified certain indicators that I call Star Indicators. These indicators seem to be more definite and easier to interpret than a lot of other indicators. So, I will discuss these indicators first in the following.

4.1 Star Indicators

The following indicators I think are the most important for the stock trader to be aware of.

4.2 The Federal Reserve Board of Governors Principle Economic Indicators

First of all, you should be aware of one the most useful sites for economic data, and that is the Federal Reserve. There is a large amount of data available from the FRB and you should spend some time studying the various statistics that they present on their web sites. The most useful data I think is found at their statistics site. You can get there by using Google and just searching on the Federal Reserve Board or you can go directly to the statistics site at http://www.federalreserve.gov/econresdata/releases/statistics data.htm

There is a lot of data at the above site including Consumer Credit, Industrial Production Capacity and Utilization, and Money Stock Measures. Of these statistics, I find Industrial Production statistics the most interesting. Select the category and then scroll down to the charts and tables.
A dip in industry production can often signal a coming recession.

The measure of M1 under Money Stock Measures also seems to be an indicator of bad economic conditions by slight decreases in the M1 money supply before a recession starts, but I cannot claim this because the effect is small and it may not be a general indicator of a recession.

4.3 The Yield Curve

The Yield Curve is published every day in the *Wall Street Journal*. It shows the yield of US government bonds vs. the time to maturity. You should calculate the difference of the ten- year Treasury bond yield and the 3-month T-bill yield. The greater the yield of the ten- year relative to the 3-month T-bill is, the less likely a recession is in the coming year. If the yields are equal (the difference is zero) there is a 25% chance of a recession in the coming year. If the difference is actually negative, the chances of a recession in the coming year increase, and the more negative it is the greater the chance of a recession is.

At a difference of minus 2.5%, the probability of a coming recession is approximately 90%. If the difference is plus 1% (the ten- year bond yields 1% more than the 3-month T-bill), the chance of a recession in the coming year is approximately 7%.

What should the stock trader do if a coming recession is predicted? The trader should start shifting to less risky investments, or alternatively, if economic conditions look very bad, the trader should consider converting to cash and waiting for buying opportunities following major corrections in the market. If the market becomes very volatile there may be trading opportunities. So, if you have lots of cash available, you can take advantage of the opportunities to buy stocks on dips and sell them on highs.

4.4 Weekly Leading Index

The Weekly Leading Index predicts major market corrections such as that of 2000-2001 and 2008-2009 almost a year ahead of the drops. The index is available weekly from ECRI, the Economic Cycle Research Institute and is reported by the ECRI site BusinessCycle.com/resources.

https://www.businesscycle.com/

The index covers a number of factors including prices, money in circulation, jobs, housing, and other indicators. The WLI has a value called the Percentage Growth Rate. If this indicator starts dropping below 0%, watch it closely.

Market corrections are indicated if the index drops below about negative 5%. In 2007 the index dropped all the way to negative 10% and in 2008 the market had a major correction.

When the WLI is above 0% or a few per cent, a recession is not indicated, but don't just look at this index only! What should an investor do? The answer is the same as discussed above under the Yield Curve above. Start reducing the risk of your portfolio.

4.5 Credit Availability

Most business is not powered by cash resources but by credit. When credit dries up, you can expect that the economy is in for a recession or a drop in business activity, loss of jobs, and possible failures of banks and other firms.

The latest example was in 2008 when we had the Great Credit Crunch. The result was the Great Recession with the collapse of Lehman Brothers and other businesses. The credit problem forced the government to support some businesses with cash, e.g., AIG, Chrysler, and General Motors. Even with the cash support, GM eventually had to declare bankruptcy and reorganize. People who held GM bonds to the very last lost all of the money that they paid for them.

The stock market nose- dived and many people suffered large losses in their 401K and IRA plans. Unemployment climbed to approximately 10%.

There is an economic indicator called the Credit Management Index (CMI) available from the National Association of Credit Management, nacm.org.

https://nacm.org/cmi.html

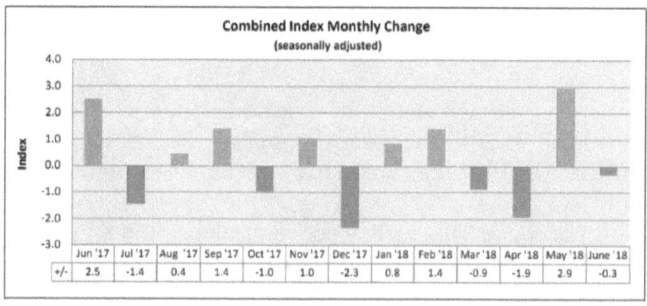

Fig. 3, The Credit Management Index

You will also find other economic data at this site including the components of the index and also the Manufacturing Index and the Service Index. The reports are explained in detail with an interpretation of the data and usually includes a statement on the outlook for the economy. This is an index that you will need to study to understand when credit availability is good or not good, but the reports themselves are very informative and will give you a very good feel for the health of the economy.

A significant drop in credit availability signals a possible recession and maybe a bear stock market as well. Take action and reduce the risk in your portfolio.

4.6 Purchasing Manager's Index

The PMI is reported by the Institute For supply Management (ISM). The link to ISM reports is www.ism.ws/ISMReport. There are a lot of great reports on this site and it's a good idea to get familiar with them.

In the case of the PMI which incorporates a lot of data that purchasing managers use to plan their purchases in the manufacturing sector. If the index drops below 50.0 it is an indication of slow manufacturing activity to come.

For example, in the year 2000 the index dropped to 49.9 in August and in 2001 the index was below 50.0 the entire year. There was a bear market in 2000 – 2001. In the year 2007, the index dropped below 50.0 in January and again in December. In 2008 the index dropped all the way down to 33.3 in December. We all know what happened in 2008.

This index is not infallible. In 1987, the index did not show any reaction, but maybe correctly. There was not a recession in 1987, but the stock market did have a massive drop that year, but there was not a recession until 1991. If you see this index drop below 50.0 it may be time to trim your portfolio and reduce risk.

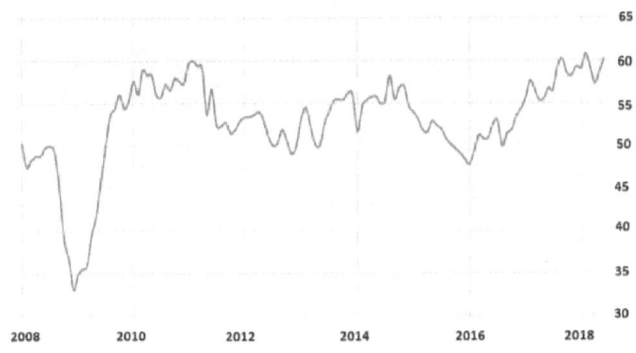

United States ISM Purchasing Managers Index (PMI)

Fig. 4, The Purchasing Managers Index (PMI)

4.7 London Interbank Offered Rate (Libor)

This index has come under some criticism for possible manipulation, so caution is in order when using this index.

Libor is the interest rate in percentage terms that banks charge each other for short term unsecured loans. During times of increasing business activity when demand for credit is high, the Libor rate will rise. In a time of recession, the demand for credit falls and so the Libor rate falls. There are other factors that affect the Libor rate also such as government tightening of the money supply, and other strains on the financial system.

The Libor rate is what is known as a 'leading' indicator of recession. For example, in June of 2006 the rate suddenly flattened out a little over 5%. Then in December of 2007 the rate suddenly dropped to approximately 3%. The recession followed in 2008 and the rate dropped to about 0.5% in June of 2008 signaling the start of the recession.

The Libor rate is published every day by the British Bankers' Association, (BBA) but you have to be a member or have some bank affiliation. You can get the current rate, the 1- month, 3- month, and 6- month rates, at Bankrate.com.

4.8 TED Spread

The TED Spread is the 3-month Libor rate minus the 3-month T-Bill interest rate. There are numerous sites such as Bloomberg and CNBC that you can find the current TED Spread. I like a site that allows you to plot the TED Spread over various time periods. One such site is:

http://www.wikinvest.com/rate/TED_Spread

When the TED spread rises over about 75 basis points it is time to expect some problems in the economy. In June of 2007 the TED shot up to almost 250 basis points and oscillated between approximately 70 to 225 basis points to June of 2008. This was one whole year of erratic behavior. It then seemed to be starting to settle down but in September of 2008, the TED spiked to over 450 basis points during the height of the credit crunch. Then it dropped back down to about 100 basis points in December of 2008. The TED then dropped down to about 50 basis points in March of 2009.

Interestingly, in March of 2009 the stock market hit a low point in 2009. When you see the TED rising strongly, it is time to think about the possibility of a recession or financial problems developing soon in the economy. So, take a look at your stock portfolio and take action to reduce risk and possibly increase your cash position to be ready for buying opportunities.

4.9 Durable Goods Orders

Durable Goods Orders can be an indicator of future business activity. However, you need to be careful in looking at the data because it can be distorted by aircraft orders and big defense orders such as an aircraft carrier.

The best indicator to use is *consumer* durable goods orders. You can find data on durable goods orders at various sites. Here is one that has historical data comparing consumer durable goods orders to S&P closing prices:

http://www.advisorperspectives.com/dshort/updates/Durable-Goods-Orders.php

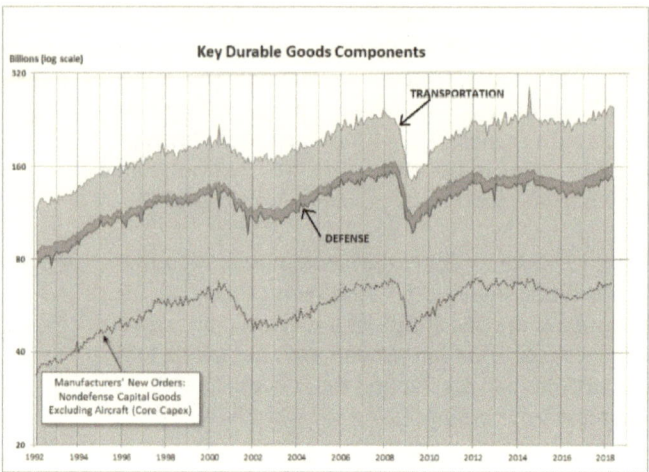

Fig. 5, Key Durable Consumer Goods Orders.

The government site census.gov also has a lot of data on the subject but it is harder to analyze it.

The main thing about durable goods orders is that as soon as a drop is noted in consumer durable goods orders of approximately 5% or more you can expect an immediate decline in the stock market and an imminent recession in the making. It is a good indicator but it is more of a coincident indicator than a leading indicator. You will not have a lot of time from the time you note a drop in durable goods orders, the occurrence of a drop in the stock market, and the onset of a recession.

4.10 Consumer Sentiment

Consumer Sentiment, also called Consumer Confidence, is a great leading indicator of recessions. It is also one of the most important indicators. If consumers lack confidence in the economy it is like they freeze. They don't buy anything they don't really need. They cut everything they can out of their expenses, such as magazines, newspapers, and sometimes even television and cell phone service.

I have heard of unemployed people living in their homes without any electric power because they either can't pay their electric bill or don't want to. In 2011, consumer sentiment was at an all- time low. Why? Because of business uncertainty, unemployment, fear of losing their job, political dissension, and a lot of other negative factors that affect their perception of the state of the economy. This is like a self-fulfilling prophecy.

It will take good government leadership to break the cycle. There is a sharp and deep drop in the CS just before a recession is about to happen. It gives you a little time to react and rearrange your portfolio of investments. Data is available from the University of Michigan.

http://www.sca.isr.umich.edu/

Again, if you see Consumer Sentiment dropping quickly, start reducing risk in your portfolio and stockpile some cash to be ready for buying opportunities.

4.11 US National Unemployment Rate

The unemployment rate is another index that will indicate when the economy is starting into a recessionary period. If we have low unemployment, under 4% to 5%, we are not in a recession, but once unemployment reaches about a 6% level, we are usually moving into a recession and it is time to expect that a market downturn is imminent. You can get a historical perspective on unemployment that shows unemployment over a period of the last 60 years at the following link:

http://forecastchart.com/graph-unemployment-rate.html

This is another indicator that will not allow you much time to react. So, if you use it, you must watch it closely. One interesting observation is that whenever unemployment drops to a minimum on the chart, there is a likely major correction in the stock market coming. The dips have occurred just before major stock market downturns of 1972, 1987, 2000, and 2008. The minimums are then followed by a sharp increase in unemployment! In 2018, it appears that another low is developing.

Fortunately, the unemployment data it is what I call a relatively smooth indicator so you can see major moves rather well if you keep up with it.

One thing to keep in mind with a rapid and heavy increase in unemployment is that there is a danger of deflation of the economy. If deflation is indeed occurring, you should reduce equities and commodity- based investments in your portfolio. Cash and cash related investments will be king. That is as prices of goods and services drop, people who have cash will have a better chance of surviving without having to stand in the soup lines.

Another thing to keep in mind is that if the economy and the financial system become extremely bad, or there is some major disaster where electric power is lost for a long time, you may not be able to get money from your bank, so it is a good idea to keep some cash at home or someplace safe where you can get it without having to go to a bank or other financial institution.

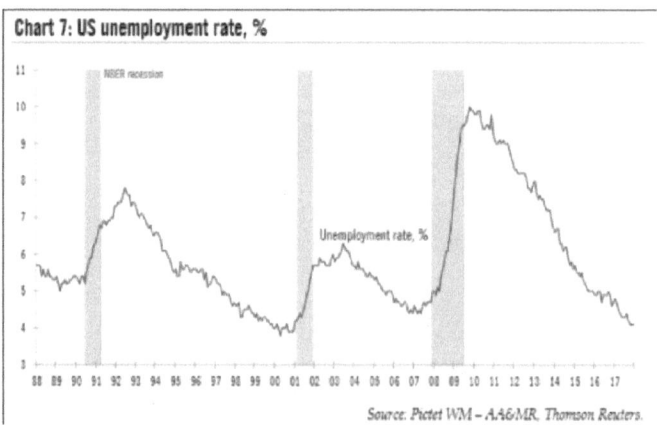

Fig. 6, US Unemployment Rate.

4.12 Tankan Survey

The Tankan Survey is an excellent leading indicator of economic activity. The TS is actually composed of four components which are separately tracked. The TS is available from the Bank of Japan. Using the link below you can find the Tankan Survey results conveniently graphed for you. Look first for the BOJ Time-Series Data. Then click on the little icon for Tankan. Then find the BOJ Long-Term Time-Series Data. You should find a four-color chart with historical data. Each color represents a part of the survey. The four components are as follows:

Large Manufacturing
Large Non-manufacturing
Small Enterprises Manufacturing
Small Enterprises Non-manufacturing

To use the survey, you should watch all of the components. When one or more of the components start to peak and start downward, it is almost always the start of a new recession. From the chart at the link below, you will see that the Tankan survey for large manufacturing shows downturns starting at the years 1985, 1991, 1996, 2000, and 2007. Of these downturns you can see the dates 1985, 2000, and 2007 precede the market downturns that follow with a year or two.

Well, you say, 'Who cares what happens in Japan?' The fact is that what happens to the economy in Japan, at least historically, also happens in the USA. Don't fight it—use it! This is one of the best economic indicators you can find.

What should you do if the Tankan survey shows the economy is about to tank? (pun intended) Again, reduce the risky components in your portfolio and build a strong cash position to be ready for buying opportunities after major market downturns.

http://www.stat-search.boj.or.jp/index_en.html

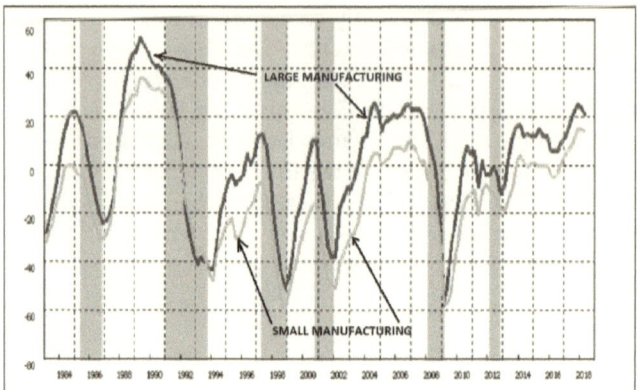

Fig. 7, The Tankan Survey.

4.13 Housing Starts

Housing Starts is an excellent indicator of pending recessions. As soon as you see housing starts leveling off or showing a significant drop off, you can expect a recession to come soon. It appears that housing starts zoom up in non-recession periods, peak out, and then start to drop. Of course, when housing starts drop this affects a lot of manufacturers, in a lot of different industries such as building materials, plumbing, electrical equipment, heating and air conditioning units, demand for copper, appliances, carpeting, etc.

A drop in housing starts also results in less demand for labor such as carpenters, electricians, plumbers, brick layers, and other personnel in the building trades. Once unemployment starts to increase due to the drop in housing starts, jobless people will buy less and this in turn affects retail stores, new automobile sales, etc. Add to the job loss, the loss of orders for building materials and you have the makings of a recession!

Why do housing starts drop in the first place? It is mainly due to consumer sentiment (see above) which is in turn a result of the strength of the economy, earnings, ease of obtaining a mortgage, interest rates, and many other factors.

There are a number of sites that have data on housing starts. The following site is the easiest site I have found to search for the data:

http://forecastchart.com/graph-housing-starts.html

Looking at the chart at the above link we can see that housing starts took a precipitous fall about 2005 and then hit a minimum in 2008. So, in this case the housing starts statistics predicted the stock market decline and the Great Recession starting at 2008.

When you see housing starts falling, it is time to dump commodity related investments, housing stocks, and most manufacturing stocks. Reduce risk in your portfolio and build up cash for buying opportunities.

Housing Starts - Annual Percentage Change

Year	Percent	Year	Percent	Year	Percent	Year	Percent
1960	-18%	1976	32%	1992	19%	2008	-33%
1961	4%	1977	28%	1993	8%	2009	-39%
1962	11%	1978	2%	1994	12%	2010	6%
1963	9%	1979	-14%	1995	-6%	2011	4%
1964	-3%	1980	-24%	1996	8%	2012	28%
1965	-5%	1981	-16%	1997	0%	2013	6%
1966	-21%	1982	-4%	1998	10%	2014	5%
1967	10%	1983	61%	1999	2%	2015	10%
1968	17%	1984	4%	2000	-4%	2016	7%
1969	-1%	1985	-1%	2001	2%	2017	2%
1970	-3%	1986	4%	2002	7%		
1971	42%	1987	-10%	2003	8%		
1972	16%	1988	-9%	2004	5%		
1973	-13%	1989	-7%	2005	6%		
1974	-35%	1990	-13%	2006	-13%		
1975	-13%	1991	-16%	2007	-26%		

Table 1, Housing Starts

4.14 Philadelphia Fed Business Outlook Survey

The Fed Business Outlook Survey is another great leading indicator of economic conditions in the future. This indicator shows sharp drops in its 'General' index before almost every recession.

You can obtain present day and historical data from the Philadelphia Fed Reserve website. The links below will allow you to find the survey data.

http://www.philadelphiafed.org/research-and-data/regional-economy/business-outlook-survey/

Go here for charts:

https://www.philadelphiafed.org/research-and-data/regional-economy/business-outlook-survey/charts

Again, watch survey data and look for sharp drops in business activity. If you see that happen, start reducing risk in your portfolio and build up cash reserves for possible buying opportunities after the stock market makes major downward moves.

4.15 S&P 500 PE Ratio

One of the most important indicators for investors is the S&P 500 PE Ratio. This ratio is a measure of the overall price to earnings ratio for the 500 S&P index stocks. The chart appears to indicate that once the ratio exceeds approximately 16, it is likely that a serious stock market correction is in the offing.

For example, in 1929 the index was 30 just before the crash. In 1987 the index was at 17 just before black Monday. In 2000 the index actually hit 43 before that bubble burst. Then when the crash of 2008 started the index was approximately

27. There are a number of good sites for this indicator. The following site has a nice historical chart:

http://www.multpl.com/

4.16 Crack Spread

This is not necessarily an economic indicator, but if you are interested in investing in a cyclical industry with a buy low and sell high technique, or buying and selling gasoline futures, you might want to look at gasoline refining. The Crack Spread is a measure of the profitability of refining (cracking) crude oil into gasoline and other petroleum products. When the spread is low it is not very profitable to refine crude oil into gasoline. When the spread is high it is more profitable.

You can find Crack Spread data at the following site and many others:

https://www.hsno.com/energy-services/crack/

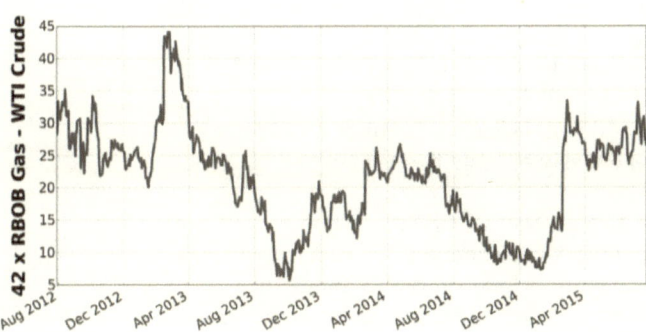

Fig. 8, The Crack Spread.

RBOB stands for **R**eformulated (Gasoline) **B**lendstock for **O**xygen **B**lending.

4.17 Volatility Index

The CBOE, Chicago Board Options Exchange, maintains an index called the Volatility Index or VIX. This index goes up in value when people believe that the stock market is about to suffer a downward move, or fears about the economy are high.

The VIX will make daily movements that are opposite to the market. You can get quotations on the VIX at any time from various services that provide stock quotes like Google, Yahoo, Bloomberg, and others.

Some people believe that the VIX is a leading indicator for the economy. It does appear that if the VIX is at or above 30 that a recession is in the near future. However, it is a fast-changing statistic and it so it should be followed daily.

The VIX index itself is not investable, but you can actually make short term investments in various VIX ETF's (exchange traded funds). Some of the symbols for these ETF's are the VXX, VIIX, VIIZ, VZZ, TVIX (2X), TVIZ (2X). The parenthetical annotation 2X means that the fund is leveraged and will move approximately two times the VIX both up and down. Usually, 2X funds should not be held more than one day or large losses may be experienced.

There are also inverse VIX ETF's that move in the opposite direction of the VIX. These are XXV, XIV, and ZIV. Another category is long/short VIX funds such as the XVIX. All of these funds should be considered to be very risky and are generally not used except by professional investors.

Some brokers will not let you buy any 2X type investments except by special permission. ProShares has a number of 2X and even 3X funds.

Fig. 9, The VIX vs. the S&P 500.

4.18 TIPS Spread

TIPS stands for Treasury Inflation Protected Securities. The TIPS Spread is an indicator of how much inflation investors expect to see in the near future. For example, if TIPS are yielding 3% and ten- year Treasury Bonds are yielding 5%, then the expected inflation is 2%.

If you expect inflation to prevail in the economy, which it has over many decades, except during the Great Depression, you should investigate buying TIPS for a relatively stable component of your investment portfolio.

The TIPS Spread is not a very good indicator of recessions in general, but the yield of TIPS actually hit 0% in 2008. The prospect of serious deflation loomed in 2008 and it was avoided only by massive business rescues and stimulus by Presidents Bush and Obama.

In deflationary periods, the coupon rate will be reduced according to the amount of deflation, and in inflationary periods the coupon will be increased by the amount of inflation, but at maturity it will still pay out its face amount of $1000.

There are many sites where you can find data on the TIPS Spread. The following site shows a good chart of the TIPS Spread vs. The S&P 500.

http://www.crossingwallstreet.com/archives/2011/08/sp-500-vs-10-year-tips-spread.html

The increase in the 10-year TIPs spread closely matches the rebound in the stock market. The TIPs spread is the difference between the 10-year Treasury yield and the yield on the inflation-protected yield. In other words, it's the market's view of expected inflation.

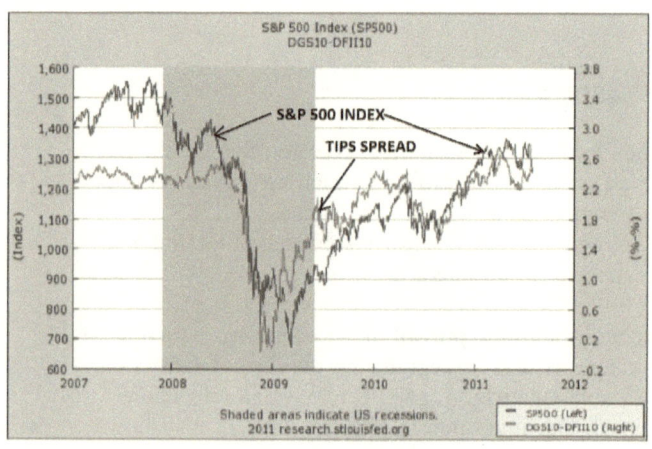

Fig. 10, The TIPS Spread vs. The S&P 500.

4.19 US Non-Farm Payroll

The non-farm payroll statistics (this is jobs, not money paid on payrolls) are not particularly valuable to the investor as this indicator is coincident and not leading. However, the statistic contributes to the fear factor in that everyone gets excited and the market will suffer a bad day if the data shows a sudden shift to zero or a negative value in a given month. Negative values are jobs lost. The non-farm payroll has been averaging approximately 200 thousand since recovery from the 2008 recession. Here is a link where you can get a good chart of historical data:

http://www.tradingeconomics.com/united-states/non-farm-payrolls

Fig. 11, US Non-Farm Payroll.

4.20 Wrapping up Economic Indicators

In Chapter 4 we discussed a number of economic indicators that I selected which should be of interest to investors. You should not just watch one indicator that you like because no one indicator will always give you the data or guidance you need.

You need to follow several indicators and watch for what I call 'indicator coincidence', that is when several indicators are forecasting a recession. In this case you will have a higher confidence that the prediction of a recession in the near future is probably accurate.

Periodically it is good to study as many indicators as you can to maintain your knowledge of economic trends and adjust your investment portfolio accordingly. But don't be a victim of data overload, where you can get confused by trying to absorb to much information at one time. Rather, take your time to carefully study and think about what you learned.

5.0 Chapter 5 Trading Methods

In this chapter we will cover only some of the many methods of stock market investing. I will cover what I think are typical methods that individual investors use, but not the very sophisticated methods that professionals might use and that are beyond the scope of this book. Some methods of trading I will only mention briefly, but if the reader is interested, I recommend doing a search on Google or Amazon.com for more information. There is a very large literature base available on stock market investing that you can access.

5.1 Asset Allocation

There are many different theories and methods as to how you should allocate your capital to achieve the best results over a lone period of time. Generally, you have stocks, bonds, and cash in your portfolio.

One theory, supported by some data, is that the best allocation of investments is a so-called balanced portfolio where you have an equal amount of capital allocated to stocks as you do to bonds to have the best returns over the long run. This is a good method for a long- term 401K plan or an IRA that you might have.

In your stock portfolio, it is good to allocate your investments between different categories of stocks. Different stock categories perform the best in any given year. Some categories you might want to include in your stock portfolio are as follows:

Large cap core equity
Large cap growth

Large cap value
Large cap dividend
Mid-cap equity
Mid-cap value
Mid-cap growth
Small cap equity
Small cap value
Small cap growth
International stocks
Emerging markets
High income stocks
Real estate investment stocks
Banks
Insurance stocks

The list of investments is practically endless with new categories emerging all the time.
If a person had unlimited funds to invest, then you could split up your investments between a lot of different categories. But when you don't have unlimited funds, you could only do this in a practical fashion by investing in either mutual funds or exchange traded funds (ETFs.)

Before you start your investment program, or if you are reorganizing your portfolio, you should spend some time researching asset allocation techniques. A complete treatment of this subject is beyond the scope of this book. The following site is a good place to start your research:

http://www.sec.gov/investor/pubs/assetallocation.htm

5.2 Dollar Cost Averaging

Anyone who is investing in the stock market can use Dollar Cost Averaging as a method of accumulating stocks at a reasonable average price over a long period of time. Now with electronic trading, you can invest easily with odd lots where you are investing a fixed amount of money, assuming you will buy at least one share of the stock you want to invest in.

For example, say that you have $100 each month extra cash that you want to invest towards building a nest egg for retirement. If you work for a company that provides the opportunity to join a 401K plan or a company stock investment plan with periodic deductions from your pay check, you should participate. These plans provide an easy way to invest and they are by their nature dollar cost averaging plans.

The way dollar cost averaging works is that with a fixed amount of cash invested on a periodic basis, you will buy more shares when the price is low and you will buy fewer shares when the price is high. So, over a long period of time, your average cost per share will probably be below the current market price assuming that you have a good investment plan.

You can establish an account with a mutual fund on your own as part of your normal savings plan, or as part of an IRA plan where you can claim tax credits of up to a certain value each year. Just call or write the mutual fund and ask for a prospectus and an account form. You don't need a stock broker. You can find good mutual funds by using a mutual fund screener. Yahoo has a good screener. You want to find funds that have had a total return of at least 3% over the past 5 or 10 years.

Also, you only want to invest in mutual funds that have expense ratios of less than 1%. The lower the expense ratio, the better. Also avoid funds that require paying an up-front commission. You should buy 'No-load' funds or 'Class C' funds that do not have an up-front commission requirement.

Also, don't buy funds that require commissions when you sell the fund. There are many good No-Load funds and you will be able to buy funds that are well diversified over many industries. Most funds specialize in certain categories, for example, small cap, mid cap, large cap, balanced, bonds, and tax- exempt securities.

A balanced fund is one that tries to maintain a 50-50 ratio between bonds and stocks, the theory being that if stocks are not doing well bonds are and vice versa. There are also so-called sector funds that specialize in certain industries such as health sciences, etc. Such funds are for the investor that is willing to take higher risk.

There are many other types of funds that the reader can research before buying. Always be careful to fully research any fund or stock before you invest.

One problem with mutual funds is that taxes are a little more complicated in that the IRS requires annual capital gains in your mutual fund account to be reported and some taxes may be due each year depending on the performance of the funds in your account.

In addition to mutual funds, there are also Exchange Traded Funds or ETF's. The disadvantage of ETF's is that you have to buy by shares instead of dollar amounts and you have to trade them through a stock broker, so it is more difficult to do dollar cost averaging. However, you can buy odd lots of most ETF's. Otherwise, the advantage of ETF's is that expenses are very small. The taxes on ETF gains are simple just like stocks. Taxes are only due when you sell a fund and have a capital gain.

You can also do dollar cost averaging with individual stock purchases with the same procedure, assuming you can buy at least one share of the stock you like.

By the way, if you have not started to save and invest for your retirement yet, you need to start as soon as possible and save as much as you can each month. I recommend at least 10% of your income each pay period, and 20% if you can.

We cannot depend on the government anymore for our retirement and medical expenses. Here are some mutual funds that illustrate the basic mutual fund characteristics you will find. The '5 yr return' per cent is the average return per year over a 5-year period. 'Cap' is short for capitalization, or the reported amount of assets a company has that the fund invests in. I list these funds only as examples, and not as recommendations to buy or sell:

USATX USAA Tax Exempt Intermediate-Term 5 yr return 4.65%
RPBAX T. Rowe Price Balanced Fund 5 yr return 5.22%
PRWCX T. Rowe Price Capital Appreciation Fund 5 yr return 6.31%
TRBCX T. Rowe Price Blue Chip Growth Fund 5 yr return 3.19%
PRDMX T. Rowe Price Diversified Mid Cap Growth 5 yr return 6.78%
PRDSX T. Rowe Price Diversified Small Cap 5 yr return 8.21%
PRHSX T. Rowe Price Health Sciences Fund 5 yr return 11.27%
PRMTX T. Rowe Price Media and Telecommunications Fund 5 yr return 12.55%

Here are some ETF's that are rated five-star by Morningstar based on performance:

QQQ   Invesco QQQ Trust (a NASDAQ index fund.)

IJT   iShares S&P small cap

QTEC   First Trust NASDAQ 100

DGRW   Wisdom Tree US quality dividend

SOXX   iShares PHLX semiconductor

CFO   Victory Shares US 500

FTCS   First Trust Capital Strength

KBWY   Invesco KBW premium yield

WOOD   iShares Global Timber

DXJS   Wisdom Tree Japan hedged small cap

The above funds that I list are by no means necessarily the "best" funds you can invest in. It is only a small listing of great and maybe better funds that are available to the investor. It is best if you do your own research to find the funds you like. You can use screeners from the yahoo.com finance page and others.

5.2.1 Small lot investing

Another way to invest is by doing what I call "small lot investing" on a regular basis. This is a good way to invest in the volatile "high technology" large capital growth stocks, sometimes referred to as the FANG, namely **F**acebook, **A**mazon, **N**etflix, and **G**oogle.

The FANG stocks are high priced stocks that makes it difficult for the small retail investor it difficult to buy 100 shares of each one. But using small lot investing you could buy say 1 share of each stock, each month until you reached some target for your total investment.

For example, let's say you want to buy one share of each company over a period of time of say three years, making purchases when you could in the FANG. Each time you would need to invest approximately $3400 according to the total shown below. Now if you wanted to invest a total of approximately $10,000, then you would buy stock at approximately one- year intervals, or more frequently if you have the cash available to do so.

Of course, the prices of the stocks could increase during the 3 years, so you would have to be prepared to invest more at each subsequent time you invested. I know this method would take a lot of patience, but I think it is better than making one large lump sum investment which is riskier in the event of a major stock market downturn, or even a bear market!

At the time I am writing this the rounded prices of the stocks are as follows:

Facebook $195
Amazon $1700
Netflix $365
Google $1140

Total = $3400

Now we have discussed the small lot investing method using the FANG stocks, *but it should be realized that the above investment (if that is all you invest in) is not diversified, is not balanced in a money-wise fashion, and does have a considerable amount of risk.*

Let us consider another approach to small lot investing. Suppose you wish to invest about $500 a month buying small lots of stock, and you want to be reasonably balanced money-wise (approximately the same amount of money is invested in each stock), and you want to have a reasonable amount of diversification across various industries. Consider the following list of stocks as an example of a small lot investment portfolio. I do not necessarily recommend these stocks! This is only an example of what could be invested in:

ACHC	Acadia Healthcare	$41	Health care
ADC	Agree Realty	$54	Real Estate
AEE	Ameren Corp.	$56	Electric util.
AIR	AAR Corp.	$48	Aerospace
APOG	Apogee Enterprises	$45	Building mat.
AWR	American States Water	$55	Water util.
AZZ	AZZ Inc.	$45	Machinery
BFS	Saul Centers Inc.	$50	Retail
BKI	Black Knight	$53	Paper
CBS	CBS Corp.	$55	Media

Table 2, Example of Small Lot Investing.

In the above list I have tried to achieve the following:

1. Diversification
2. Price greater than $40 per share (for quality)
3. P/E 0 – 20
4. EPS = > $1 per share

You may calculate that the average price per stock of the above list is $50.20. So, if you bought one share of each stock each month, you would be investing approximately $500 each month. If you want to invest $1000 a month, then buy two shares of each stock, and so on. This is another way to apply "small lot investing" (SLI.) To find the above list I used the free stock screener, FINVIZ:

https://finviz.com/

5.3 Lump Sum Investing

If you have a lump sum to invest, you need to be careful that you do not buy just one stock and get pinned to a high price for that stock that could be a persistent loss for you if the market or the stock moves lower by a significant amount.

It would be safer to do one of the following:

(1) Divide your sum into 5 to 10 portions and wait to invest each portion, one at a time, at equal time periods over at least several months or even better, over one or two years.

(2) Do the same as (1) but invest each portion only on market down days. (Don't put money into a market that is in free fall however.)

(3) Do the same as (1) but invest your funds in 5 to 10 or more different stocks in different industries to diversify your investment.

(4) Do the same as (1) but invest in 5 to 10 or more different categories of mutual funds or ETF's to develop a highly diversified portfolio, depending on how much money you have to invest.

(5) Do the same as (1) but invest in 5 to 10 high income dividend paying stocks that will provide you income from your lump sum.

If you are new to investing, make sure you get professional advice before investing, but don't let anyone talk you into making one particular investment. Don't listen to rumors about "hot stocks". Do your own research if you can. A good free stock screener is finviz.com.

Sometimes in less reputable investment firms, brokers will be told to "push" certain stocks. If you suspect that this is happening, close your account and find a more reputable broker.

5. 4 Short Term Trading

If you are in a position where you have saved some extra money (not funds that you have invested for the long term for retirement), you may want to trade stocks for short term profits. This is not an easy thing to do however, especially if there is a bear market for stocks which it usually is during recessionary periods.

The first thing you should do is evaluate economic conditions (See Chapter 4 above) so you can get an idea what the stock market is likely to do in the near future, i.e., is the market going to be a bear market or a bull market? If the market is likely to be a bear market, you will need to be very careful to research what types of investments might be good in a bear market and have enough volatility for you to buy and sell with profits.

Even if the economic indicators are not signaling a recession, you still need to careful because even if the market as a whole is a bull market, certain stocks or investments may be moving into their own little bear market.

Most types of good stocks do well in a bull market, but not many will do well in a bear market. Of course, there are investments that do better in a bear market than in a bull market, such as inverse funds, gold, puts and other investments we will describe later.

But for now, lets assume that you foresee a bull market. Then what kinds of stocks can you expect to trade for profits? In a bull market, technology stocks generally do the best, but you need to find some that have good fundamentals

(See Chapter 3) but are volatile. That is, they move down fast on day when the market is down, and they move up fast on a day when the market is up.

You can use a stock screener to find stocks that have good fundamentals, but have high beta, and large volume resulting in volatility. Once you have found a group of stocks that meet your criteria, you should study their charts and try to determine whether their stock price has a somewhat cyclical nature.

Sometimes you will be able to plot two straight lines on their charts. One line connects the high points, and one line connects the low points. So, the upper line will allow you to predict the next high point and the lower line will allow you to predict the next low point.

Now the trick is to buy the stock at or close to a low point and then sell when the stock is at or close to a high point. Once a stock nears a low point, wait for a 'down' day in the market and buy the stock. Then if the stock gets near its high point, wait for an 'up' day in the market to sell the stock.

When I do short term trading, I look for my stocks to increase by at least 10% to 15% before I sell. In short term trading, you should also set a downside limit of some percentage you can tolerate. I like a -10% downside limit before I sell a stock (only if it is a short- term trade.)

Professionals usually sell with a -7% downside limit. You could also enter a "stop-loss" order at say -7% or -10% if you have a very volatile market situation and there is reason to believe that a bear market is imminent.

If you want to, you can read any number of books on technical chart analysis which is a very complex study. I prefer the more simplified approach I just described. You should shoot for situations that will provide 10% to 15% profit. You need to have enough profit to pay the stock trading commissions and to cover the time you have spent analyzing the stocks, etc. After all, your time is worth some money. Isn't it?

The following is a list of stocks that have a PE of 15 or less and are either volatile or have a steady growth pattern. I found these stocks by using the Yahoo stock screener and I am presenting these stocks only as examples to research, not as recommendations to buy or sell. This is not an exhaustive list:

OZRK	Bank of the Ozarks
KRO	Kronos Worldwide
CLF	Cleveland Cliffs
WDR	Waddell and Reed Financial
UVE	Universal Insurance
ECPG	Encore Capital Group
NL	NL Industries
PERY	Perry Ellis International
VEC	Vectrus
OSG	Overseas Shipholding Group
NHTC	Natural Health Trends
KODK	Eastman Kodak

Table 3, Stocks with PE of 15 or less

5.5 Cyclical Stocks

Another method of short-term trading which is really closer to long term trading, is to find stocks in cyclical industries that are priced lower at low points in their business cycle and priced higher at their high points in their business cycle. There are a number of cyclical stocks that you will be able to find if you do the research. Below are the stocks in the Morgan Stanley Cyclical Stock Index, CYC. I present these stocks only as examples and not as a recommendation to buy or sell. You should do your own research before investing.

AA Alcoa
CAT Caterpillar
C Citigroup
CSX CSX Corp.
DE Deere & Co.
DD Dupont
ETN Eaton
FDX FDX Corp.
F Ford Motor
GT Goodyear Tire & Rubber
HON Honeywell
IR Ingersoll-Rand
IP International Paper*
JCI Johnson Controls*
MAS Masco Corp.
MMM 3M
PPG PPG Industries
R Ryder Systems**
UTX United Technologies
X USX-US Steel Corp.
WHR Whirlpool Corp.*

 * Excellent for trading cycles
 ** Very low P/E
Table 4, Cyclical Stocks

5.6 Day Trading

Day trading is one of the riskiest trading techniques that people do. Very few people are successful at day trading. It is more like gambling than investing. The day trader is trying to predict if a stock will move up during the day (or down if he is selling short) and usually has to buy a lot of shares of the stock to make a significant profit if it does.

So, the day trader has to have a lot of capital to work with that he is willing to risk on one or only a few stocks with maybe a 50-50 or less chance of making a profit. He will have little information to support his decision to invest other than maybe the stock is on a move when he decides to buy it.

Let's take an example. Suppose the trader has $50,000 to invest in a day trade. He finds stock XYZ that costs $50 per share and is starting to move upward. So, the trader buys 1000 shares. The stock moves up $0.10 a share but then just hangs there the rest of the day. Because the trader does not want to hold his position overnight, he sells his 1000 shares for $50.10 each.

On paper he has made $100 on the day. But wait, his commission he has to pay is 1% of the total to buy or sell. So, his commission to buy is $500 and another $500 to sell. So, the trader has a net loss of $900 for the day. If the trader has a special account with only a 0.1% commission or $50 per trade, then he is breakeven for the day.

Of course, there is a chance that the stock will move up $1 or more on a good day, but there is no way to know that for sure in advance. By the way, the day trader will have to have a special account with a broker because brokerage firms don't allow just anybody to do day trading.

Normally, brokers want 3 days to settle any stock transaction which makes day trading not really their normal way of doing business. I don't recommend day trading for the average investor.

5.7 Buy and Hold

Buying and holding stocks for the long term is out of favor as I am writing this. I think the reason is that stocks have been taking a beating for two-thirds of a decade and people are kind of suffering from a sort of shell shock looking at the losses they have because they bought the wrong stocks.

I think 'buy and hold' is still one of the best methods of investing, provided that a person does his research and buys only high- quality stocks with good prospects for the future. Statistics are on my side. The statistics show that long term investors that don't buy and sell just because the market goes up or down, do better in the long run than people who are always trying to time the market and sell when things look bad.

That is not to say that you should not sell a stock if it has gone south or has developed some fatal flaws. You do have to watch your stocks and watch the news on them so that you can sell the ones that do go bad occasionally. This is a different reason for selling than just selling stocks because the overall market is up or down.

Some people even do the worst sort of trading by buying when the market is high and then selling out when the market has already dropped because they are frightened. These people guarantee trading loses by doing that.

If you like to trade in and out of the market, then buy when stocks are low and sell when stocks are high, if you have a reasonable profit. The person who buys good stocks and holds them for the long term will have an average return over a long period of 10% to 12% per year, according to the statistics.

That is a very good return for doing nothing other than some research and investing some capital. What are some good stocks to consider for long term investing? I present a list here from using a stock screener with some fairly tight criteria. The criteria I used are Beta <= 1.0, PE <=20, ROE (return on equity) >=15, ROA (return on assets)>= 1.0%, and Profit Margin >= 10%.

From the screener results, I further selected North American stocks only and companies that I am familiar with. The stocks are listed in order of decreasing market capitalization. I present this list as examples of high-quality stocks, not as recommendations to buy or sell. You should do your own research.

MSFT Microsoft Corp.
IBM International Business Machines
CVX Chevron
KO Coca-Cola
MMM Minnesota Mining and Manufacturing
ABX Barrick Gold
LLY Eli Lilly
NGG National Grid
NEM Newmont Mining
EXC Exelon
GIS General Mills
RCI Rogers Communications
NLY Annaly Capital
PEG Public Service Enterprise Group

Table 5, Stocks for long term investment.

5.71 401K Plan Investing

If you have a 401K plan available to you, it is a great way to invest. Your employer usually contributes a percentage to your plan if you contribute. Sometimes the employer may contribute as much as 25% of your salary to your plan. The plan is also portable so you can change jobs and use it at your next job again. Sometimes you are limited to certain funds and a certain brokerage house to invest with but it is still a great way to invest for retirement.

5.72 Retirement plan called an IRA

When you do retire, you can 'roll it over' your 401k plan into an IRA which is again a good way to save your money and even keep buying and trading stocks. You can even do some kinds of options such as 'covered call' writing. We will discuss options in a later section.

The IRA plan is controlled by certain government regulations that must be adhered to. I will not cover such regulations here, except to mention one requirement: When you reach age 70 ½ you must start making withdrawals from your IRA plan. You can find other requirements of the IRA plan here:

https://www.irs.gov/retirement-plans/individual-retirement-arrangements-iras

Or use Google search to get the latest information.

5.8 Conservative Income Stocks

Another way you can use the Buy and Hold strategy is to also get some income from your quality stocks. When I say 'conservative' income, I mean high quality companies that have yields of at least 3.0%. Generally, high quality stocks do not have yields in excess of 7% or 8%.

Below is a list of a dozen companies that are conservative investments that pay a dividend of 3% or more. Note that the Federal Reserve targets 2% inflation so that they have some leverage to control the economy, so you need at least 3% to have a little return above inflation! I have tried to pick different industries to give a degree of diversification. It is by no means an exhaustive list!

I present this list only as examples, not as recommendations to buy or sell. Note that companies often reduce their dividends when they are under some stressful condition which is affecting their earnings. So, it is necessary to continually review your portfolio. You should do your own research.

CVX	Chevron Corp.	3.54%
KO	Coca-Cola	3.59%
NGG	National Grid	4.96%
EXC	Exelon	3.45%
GIS	General Mills	4.40%
RCI	Rogers Communications	3.19%
PEG	Public Service	3.52%
BIP	Brookfield Infrastructure	4.61%
GM	General Motors	3.45%
XOM	Exon Mobil	3.99%
T	AT&T	5.82%
MRK	Merck and Co.	3.22%

Table 6, Conservative Income Stocks.

5.9 High Income Stocks

Investing in high income stocks is a way to earn higher income with limited capital to invest. It is research intensive as you look for quality companies that have a good yield (I look for yields higher than 8.0%) and also have a low payout ratio.

In other words, the dividend is well supported by higher earnings per share. For example, suppose a company is paying a $1.00 dividend per share, but has an EPS of $1.50 has a payout ratio of 66.6%, leaving a margin of protection for the dividend payout of 33.3%.

The higher the margin of protection is, the safer the dividend is, especially when economic conditions are bad. Investing in high income stocks is like the buy and hold strategy, but you must constantly watch your high- income stocks for things like dividend reductions, drops in EPS below the dividend, operating losses, or other bad news.

It is best to put only limited funds into each stock and hold as many different high- income stocks as possible and practical for this portion of your portfolio to diversify your portfolio and have a steady income from your investments.

The best way to find good stocks for this investment strategy is to use a stock screener, and then do further research to check items that the screener does not look for, such as the payout ratio.

Below is a list of high-income stocks with high market caps and relatively low P/E. Most of them are volatile, so it is important to invest carefully. It is best to examine their charts closely and only buy at low points and with a limited amount of investment each time you buy. Do not do a major lump sum investment at one time on any one stock. Also watch them closely for changes in their dividends or bad news that will impact the price. There are many of these stocks so you can find more using a good screener such as finviz.com. I present these stocks as examples only, not as recommendations to buy or sell.

AGNC	American Capital Agency	11.42%
ARI	Apollo Commercial Real Estate	9.78%
NLY	Annaly Capital Management	11.41%
IVR	Invesco Mortgage Capital	10.21%
CIM	Chimera Investment Corp.	10.82%
MFA	MFA Financial	10.58%
CLNC	Colony Northstar Credit Real Estate	9.11%
BPL	Buckeye Partners L.P.	13.85%
EEP	Enbridge Energy Partners	13.70%
NRZ	New Residential Investment	10.98%

Table 7, High Income Stocks.

5.10 New Growth Stocks

In the New Growth category, I am talking about relatively new companies that are growing fast, have good fundamentals, good prospects for the future, and are popular with investors. One caution, however, is that such stocks tend to be very volatile and you will have to have a high tolerance for risk.

In this category, I think the best method would be a buy and hold strategy for the long run, but you could also do short term trading on the volatility. Where can you find these stocks?

One way to find these stocks is to get a copy of *The Investors Business Daily* newspaper or the online version. This source does an excellent job of researching these and other stocks and presenting the data in a timely and useful fashion along with financial news. Here is a link to the online version:

http://www.investors.com

5.11 Small Cap Stocks

Small cap stocks are a good place to invest for the long term. I believe that it is best to use an ETF or mutual fund to invest in this area because it is almost imperative that your investment in this category should be very highly diversified so that your risk is limited.

One advantage of this category is that it seems to deliver consistently good results over many decades. Of course, small cap stocks have bad years, but when they have good years, they are very good with returns in the 15% or greater area.

Here are funds that specialize in small cap and mid-cap stocks. I present these as examples only and not as recommendations to buy or sell.

OTCFX T. Rowe Price Small-Cap Stock Fund
FSLCX Fidelity Small Cap Stock Fund
VTWV   Vanguard Russell 2000 Value ETF
FNK   First Trust Mid Cap Value AlphaDEXA ETF

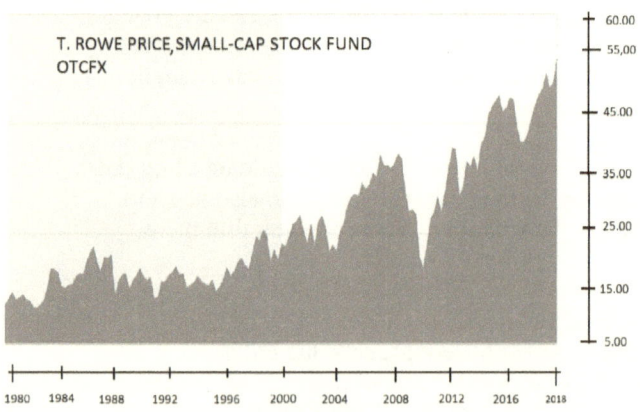

Fig. 12, Small-Cap Stock Fund.

5.12 Penny Stocks

Penny stocks are difficult to invest in because information on them is difficult to obtain. My experience with penny stocks is that at the best only about 1 in 12 penny stocks is likely to increase significantly in value. So that means that you will have to make a lot of investments with little chance of making a good hit.

If you can spend time to watch a stock ticker tape which sometimes is available on certain television channels or at some brokerage websites, if they cover penny stocks. Watch the tape for penny stocks that are active and are moving higher in price. Make note of them and then do research on them to find the best ones. I look for the ones that have significant revenue, at least some earnings, and good news articles. Read the news about the company and look for good reports and good prospects for success.

One advantage of penny stocks is that you can buy a lot of shares for a small amount of money. So, if you have some extra money it is possible you could buy enough of these kinds of stocks to eventually make a good profit on one or two. A high- risk tolerance and a lot of patience will be required.

Here is a list of examples of penny stocks that I got by using a stock screener with the simple criteria that the price is <= $1 and the PE<=20. This list is presented as examples only and is not a recommendation to buy or sell.

HGT   Hugoton Royalty Trust
CRSN   CarSmart Inc.
CGEI   CGE Energy Inc.
BSTO   Opportunities Corp. USA
USRI   Recycling Industries Inc.
TLPC   Telpac Industries Inc.
CYXV   CTX Virtual Technologies Inc.
VRSYF   VMS Rehab Systems Inc.

A much bigger list can be obtained from a screener if a higher P/E is allowed.

5.13 Emerging Markets

Investing in emerging markets is risky but the profit potential is high. There are both mutual funds and exchange traded funds available to invest in. The emerging markets are the fastest growing economies and there will be profits to be made in this category. I give a list here of some typical funds available to invest in. There are many more available besides this short list. I provide this list only as examples and not as recommendations to buy or sell.

DEMSX DFA Emerging Markets Small Cap I
EMGYX Wells Fargo Advantage Emerging Markets Eq Adm
ODVYX Oppenheimer Developing Markets
DREGX Driehaus Emerging Markets Growth
EEM MSCI Emerging Markets Index Fund (ETF)

The above funds are volatile so it is important to buy only at a low point as shown by examination of the fund price vs. time for each fund. All of the funds are rated either 4 star or 5 stars by Morningstar.

5.14 Initial Public Offerings (IPOs)

Initial Public Offerings are usually risky investments. Your chance of losing 50% of your investment in the first week after issue is very great, if you invested on the first day of issue. On the other hand, if the company that is issuing their first offering is a very profitable and popular company, you may have a winner. Some stocks have increased significantly from their first issue and have made their early investors a lot of money.

So how can you pick the right IPOs to invest in? You must do research, research, and more research. You must know the company well. You must read all the news on the company. There is no substitute for having knowledge when investing in IPOs.

5.141 High Technology Stocks

I am mentioning this category of investing because there are many important stocks in high technology that have attained very large capitalizations. For example, the so- called FANG stocks:

Facebook
Amazon
Netflix
Google

There are many stocks which are important also, the sub-categories:

Information Technology
Computers
Communications
Software
Medical devices
Semiconductors
Biotechnology
Pharmaceuticals
Robotics
Artificial intelligence
Etc.

5.142 Exchange Traded Funds

Exchange traded funds, or ETFs as they are usually referred to, are a major investment category now. The funds are usually set up to invest in certain stocks in a certain category, for example biotechnology, the S&P 500, emerging markets, bonds, semiconductors, and almost any type of stocks or investments.

The advantage of ETFs are usually low volatility compared to single stocks, relative safety, easy to research, and popular as investments. There are fees so you have to find out what the expense ratio is, usually expressed as a percentage of the amount of money you invested. Typical rates run from 0.1% to 1%. The better the performance is generally, the higher the expense ratio will be.

You should find out what the top 10 investments are that the fund is buying, and check this periodically to make sure the fund is investing the way you want it to. Also are the investments the fund is making satisfactory to your risk tolerance?

I recommend ETFs for long-term investors who are not interested in trading often but still want good growth of capital or dividends.

5.143 Miscellaneous Investment categories

There are many other methods of investment which are beyond the scope of this book, for example, real estate, commodities, precious metals, antiques, crypto currencies, collectibles, futures, and many more. I you invest in one of these categories it is advisable to first study about the categories and be sure you have enough knowledge to do so. You may have to reach out to experts to get advice or appraisals. Watch out for 'scams' and fakes!

5.15 Investment Clubs

What if you don't have time to do research? How can you find out what are "good" stocks to buy? A possible answer for you is to join a local investment club.

What is an investment club? An investment club is a group of people in a local community that gather periodically to discuss various investments, usually in the stock market. There is usually a leader or moderator that controls the meeting.

There are many ways that an investment club can operate but it might be as follows:

The moderator may ask for volunteers to give a report on certain stocks that they will research for the club. So that at each meeting a few stocks will be reported on with some fundamental or technical stock date. Then the moderator may ask for a vote from the club members as to which of the stocks reported on are the best to invest in.

After the club has decided which stocks the like for investment, club members may buy those stocks or not. There is no obligation to buy any stocks or deal with any particular broker, and no money should be collected in a free legitimate investment club. However, there may be a fee to join the club to cover any expenses that the club may incur.

5.16 Automated Trading

If you don't have any time at all to research and pick stocks and you don't have time to join an investment club, there is now another way. Consider an automated investment account now available to retail investors.

One company that provides this service is TD Ameritrade. They will provide automated trading "with low cost, low minimum" investment in a group of "five goal-oriented ETFs". I recommend going very slow on this with a test run to see how well they perform before committing a large amount of money to an account like this. Automated programs are notorious for suddenly selling you out for the slightest trigger condition.

However, if the software is good you should get good results. When the automated process is applied to ETFs instead of individual stocks, the investment should be fairly safe. You can find information here:

https://www.tdameritrade.com/investment-products/managed-portfolios.page

5.17 Churning

Don't allow a stock broker to constantly churn your account, that is, continually sell and buy stocks without regard to profit and not in your best interest. This is called "churning"!

If you suspect a broker is doing this, you can report him to his boss, and you should immediately seek compensation! If your account is not rectified, you should immediately sell all of your stocks, request a check for the full amount, and then find a new broker. I would not normally ask for stock certificates because the broker will no doubt charge you heavy fees on each certificate.

In the same way, you yourself should not sell and buy stocks all the time. Don't sell a good stock just because it has dropped a few points! More money is usually made by staying with your stocks for the long haul. You will make more money sitting on your ass than constantly selling and buying new stocks!

5.18 Re-balancing Your Portfolio

Re-balancing a portfolio is a current buzz-word that usually involves selling stocks that have even only small gains and buying new ones periodically. The problem with re-balancing is that you might give up good stocks and your portfolio becomes a collection of mediocre stocks.

My suggestion is that you should keep all of the stocks that are performing well and sell the stocks that are definitely underperforming and have no real chance of improved performance in the time frame that suits you, or are even in a bear market because of some basic fault or a weak competitive position because of the changes in consumer buying habits or obsolescence of their products.

Examples are the near collapse of Kodak when the digital cameras and smart phones came into existence. Other examples are the virtual demise of retail stores with the advent of the rise of the Amazon juggernaut. An example here is the bear market in Sears stock as they have apparently been unable to adapt to the new online marketing paradigm.

However, there is a simple thing to do if you have stocks that have doubled or more in value. Sell one-half of your shares of a stock that has doubled. You thereby recover your total investment in the stock and the rest of the shares you retain becomes a kind of "free" investment.

6.0 Chapter 6 Using Options with Stock Investments

Since the focus of this book is stock investing and not trading options alone as investments, we will not discuss all of the myriad of different methods of options investing. However, sometimes stock investors can use options to enhance their income and add a measure of protection to their investments. Before we discuss the use of options with stocks, we need to explain what stock options are and some basics of how they work.

6.1 What are stock options?

A stock option is a right, sometimes referred to as a contract, to buy or sell 100 shares of stock per option contract, of a certain stock, to buy from or sell to the option seller (writer), respectively, at a certain price called the strike price within a time period up to the expiration date.

The option is sold by an option "writer" to whoever wants to buy it, at a certain price for the option, for a certain strike price of the stock, for a certain expiration date. All stock options have set expiration dates which are usually on the third Friday of the month.

Options can be sold or bought anytime for expiration in the month, or subsequent months, up to even one, or even two years. The long- term options for one and two years are sometimes referred to a LEAPS.

Options can be 'exercised' or acted upon with an exercise order from the option owner for the stock at any time before the expiration date for American style options. European style options can only be exercised at the expiration date.

The seller of an option, also called the 'option writer', can buy back or close his option obligation at any time before expiration, simply by buying the same option strike, expiration date, and the same number of 'contracts' on the open market. This is called 'closing' a position.

Also, the buyer of an option can close his position at any time prior to expiration simply by selling his option position on the open market. Note that neither the seller nor the buyer of an option will be able to close his position at the same price that he wrote it or bought it necessarily, because he will have to buy or sell it on the options market at asked or bid price respectively which might have increased or decayed.

One options contract consists of the right to buy or sell 100 shares of the underlying stock, depending on whether the option is a 'call' or a 'put', respectively.

A call is the right to buy 100 shares for each call contract at the "strike" price from the option writer. If the price of the stock has moved up significantly above the "strike price, the owner of the call will have a large profit.

A put is the right to sell 100 shares to the put writer, respectively, both at the specified strike price within the expiration date. If the price of the stock has declined significantly below the strike price, the owner of the put will have a large profit.

Call options become more valuable if the price of the stock starts to exceed the strike price of the option. Put options become more valuable if the stock price starts to drop below the strike price. In order to take advantage of the profit, if any, the owner of the option must exercise his or her option before or on the expiration date.

6.2 Covered Calls

Brokers don't like customers to sell (write) option contracts 'naked', that is without any supporting capital or stock coverage. If a person sells a naked call and the stock rises in price dramatically, the losses to the call writer are virtually unlimited.

If the option writer cannot pay up the value of the options or supply the stock when the option contracts are called by the option buyer, then the broker is stuck with the cost and has to make it good. So, unless you are very well- heeled, the broker will not allow you to sell naked calls and puts.

But if you own 100 shares of stock XYC, you can sell one contract call option on the 100 shares as a 'covered call' because your call is backed up by your ownership of the stock. Your sale of an option contract can also be "covered" by owning a call contract on the same stock at a much lower strike price that has a longer expiration date (if your broker allows it.)

If the stock price and the call price rise dramatically, the call writer does not get hurt because the stock value has increased so the option price increases and covers the higher value.

The writer gets to keep his premium for writing the option in the first price. The money for the option he sells comes into his account the same day, or at least within three days, the maximum time within which transactions must be settled.

If the option was written as an 'out of the money call' (OTM) call, and the stock never rises above the strike price, the option will most likely not be exercised by the option owner so the premium for the call write is 100% for the option writer.

If the option was written at the same strike price as the value of the stock at the time of the option writing, it was an 'at the money' (ATM) option. The exercise of the option "at the money" and the sale of the stock will be a break-even sale. The option writer still gets to keep the premium for selling the option and so still could make a profit on the transaction, except for the cost of commissions.

This is the way a covered call option writer can make extra income on his stock if he sells the right call against his stock. So, what is wrong with doing this all the time? Nothing, except the option writer knows that if the market price of the stock declines significantly during the period, he may have a big paper loss on his stock.

The buyer of the options will most likely not exercise his options in such a case, but just let them expire. In this case the buyer of the options has a loss on the options he bought against the stock, and the option writer has a paper loss on his stock, but he still has his premium for writing the options. The premium he received reduces his net loss a little and he has the option premiums as cash in his account. He can then write new call options against his stock again and again as long as he owns his stock and it still has some value.

6.3 Example of a Covered Call Write

Let's discuss an example of a covered call write based on real data. The data I will use is based on data quoted for General Electric stock on Sept. 6th, 2011. The price of GE stock was $15.25. Suppose that we purchase 1000 shares for a total cost of $15250 plus whatever commissions and fees are applicable.

Once we are sure the order has been actually executed (be very sure about this), we will write a covered call "out of the money" (OTM) option of 10 contracts (covering 1000 shares). As we go to the options trading label in our broker's software, we search options available to write for GE stock. Since we bought the stock for $15.25 per share (or better a lower value if we dollar cost average our purchase), we may not want to give up the stock unless we get at least $16 per share for it as a reasonable expectation for this example.

So, we check the options table for calls for Sept. and we find that we can only sell a $16 strike option for 2 cents per share. That small amount would only yield us $20 for 10 contracts (10X100X$0.02=$20). So, we look further ahead in time still holding to our goal of a $16 strike. If we go out to the November options, we see that we can write a $16 strike option for $0.58 per share. This will yield us a premium of (10X100X$0.58)=$580.

So, if we write this option on our 1000 shares, writing the 10 contracts for the November $16 strike. Now if the price of GE stock goes over $16 by the third Friday in November, our stock of 1000 shares will be called for $16 per share by the option owner (this is virtually certain to happen.) Your broker will automatically transfer your shares to the call owner. Now your total profit is ($580+$750)=$1330 less your commissions.

If you could do a write like this one every 3 months of the year with that kind of return, your equivalent yearly yield would be 34.8%, less commissions. Of course, this assumes you will always pick the correct stock that will go up by at least $0.75 or $1 per share in the 3-month periods, and that your option premium will always be at least $0.58. This is not very likely and you may only have this kind of luck 50% of the time. If that is the case, your yearly yield is 17.4% which is still very good.

Now the other part of the problem is that you must be very careful to research the stocks you buy for using covered call options, checking fundamentals and news on the stocks to be as sure as possible that you are not buying into a stock that will suffer a big drop in a downturn of the market, or turn into its own bear market!

Remember that it is best to buy your stock using as close to a dollar cost averaging method as possible so that your average price is hopefully less than the current market value at the time you begin writing the options. Otherwise, if you invest in a lump sum you are taking a big risk that you will suffer a big loss if your stock drops one or two dollars during the time you have written the option.

By the way it is best to do covered call options only during times when the market is very stable or is a bull market. Not all stocks have options available to trade so you must check that point.

One other thing is that the stock must have a reasonable amount of volatility or the premiums for the options will not be very good. The price of an option is a measure of what options traders think the price of the stock will be at the end of the option period. If traders don't think the price will move much, the value of the option premium will be low and not worth writing a contract for.

6.4 Writing Put Options

Now suppose that you want to do the covered call method but you don't want to buy the GE stock at $15.25. But you would buy it if you could obtain it at $14 per share. So, you set aside at least enough money to buy 1000 shares for $14 per share in your account with your broker. This called a cash-secured put contract. Be sure to tell your broker that you intend to write a cash-secured put on the stock and get his approval to do so.

Now you look up the prices on puts for GE stock. You find an October $14 per share strike for GE has a premium of $0.49 per share. So, you write 10 put option contracts at the $14 per share strike price for October expiration. You get $490 coming into your account the same day you write the option contracts. You get to keep the premium no matter what happens.

Now if the stock drops to say $13 per share or lower, the stock will be "put" to you at $14 per share, or for a total of $14000. So, you lost $1000 on the value of your stock but you collected $490 on your put write premium so your net loss is ($14000-$13000-$490) = ($510) plus commissions, and the net cost of acquiring your shares is $14510 plus commissions.

Now you are still better off than if you had bought the stock at the market value of $15.25 where your total cost would have been $15250 plus commissions.

Now time has passed to October and now you can sell a covered call on the 1000 shares you own. If you write the call contracts for the January 2012 $16 strike options, you could collect an estimated $0.50 premium or (10X100X$0.50)=$500. So, your total profit if the stock is called is ($16000-$14510+$500) = $1990.

The yield for the 5 months is then 13.7%. If this procedure could be done over a 12 month period, your equivalent yield would be (100X13.7 / 5)X12 = 32.8% less cost of commissions. If the option is not exercised and the stock is not put to you, you have still collected $490 on the cash the broker is holding for you in your account.

If you consider the cash which is essentially impounded by the broker as long as the options are still not exercised or not expired, as your invested money, your yield is (100X$490/$14000X7 / 5) = 4.9% (about the same amount of interest you could obtain on a ten- year T-bond for 1 year.)

Clearly it is better to start a covered call operation with the cost of your stock that you bought less than the current market value by whatever investing method you used, buy and hold, dollar cost averaging, or writing put contracts.

One thing to note is that you cannot do any option trading in a 401K account, and the only options trading you can do in an IRA account is covered calls. Always be sure your broker knows what you plan to do and that he approves.

6.5 Buying Puts to Protect Stock Value

Now let's suppose that the economy looks bad and you are expecting a serious decline in market value of your GE stock or other stocks. So, you want to buy a put to protect your stock. We will use your GE stock as an example and assume it has cost you $14510. Looking again at the GE put options available to buy, you could buy a January 2012 put at a strike price of $16 for a premium cost of $2.06 per share for $2060 total for 10 contracts.

Now if in January, the stock falls to a market value of $10 per share, you "put" the stock to the put writer for $16 per share. You have not only preserved your stock value but your net transaction is ($16000-$14510-$2060)=-$570. So, you have protected your investment for $114 per month for 5 months, or 9.4% on a yearly basis. This is not bad if the market dropped 15% to 20% in which case you would probably have had a loss of more than 10% on your stock, if you had not bought the put.

On the other hand, if the value of your stock was above $16 in January, say $16.50 per share, the put would not be exercised, but your equivalent cost would now be ($16500-$14510-2060) = -$70. So, the put buy has still protected you.

6.6 Buying a Straddle

A straddle is a simple but powerful way to use options to make money whether a stock increases in value or decreases in value. The disadvantage of a straddle is that a profitable outcome may take time to develop depending on the amount of volatility of the stock and the characteristics of the options that are bought to form the position.

The basic formation of a straddle is to buy a call and a straddle on the same stock with the same strike price and expiration time. Usually we want to buy ATM ("at the money") options only for straddles and with long expiration times.

To form the straddle, we buy one put option and one call option. The chart below shows a calculation of profit or loss for a straddle on a stock at a strike price of $100 and buying an ATM call for $1 per share, and an ATM put for $1 per share with a total cost of $200 for the options position. Then calculate profit and loss for changes in the stock price of +10/-10 %.

EXAMPLE OF A STRADDLE

		INVEST COST
ATM STOCK PRICE=	100	
ATM PUT	1	100
ATM CALL	1	100
TOTAL COST	2	200

STOCK PRICES	PROFIT/LOSS
90	800
91	700
92	600
93	500
94	400
95	300
96	200
97	100
98	0
99	-100
100	-200
101	-100
102	0
103	100
104	200

105	300
106	400
107	500
108	600
109	700
110	800

Note that if the stock were to change in price by either +10% or -10%, the profit would be $800 which is a return on investment of 400%! But also note that the stock has to change up or down by at least $3 a share to have at least $100 in profit, not counting broker commissions on the transaction. This is why you need to have a volatile stock for this option position and watch it closely. You should be ready to quickly close out a position when you have a profit or the profit may evaporate with a further up or down movement in stock price.

6.7 Vertical Spreads

In the table below, we see some options listed for GE stock for expiration August 03, 2018. As an example of a vertical spread in the case, we will construct what is called a "Bear Call Spread" and a "Bull Put Spread". A bear call spread might be initiated when a trader expects a certain stock to decline in value over a period of time. A bull put spread might be initiated if a trader expects a stock to increase in value.

With the stock price at $12.85 a share on the date he initiates the spread, the trader chooses to go "short" the $13 strike (he writes or sells the option), and "long" the $13.5 strike both for expiration on Aug 03, 2018. He will have a credit in his account of ($53 -$32) = $21 less commissions per number of contracts. If he sells 10 contracts of each strike, his net credit is $210 less commissions. If the stock does not hit $13 within the expiration period, he gets to keep the net premium for the position.

If at the end of the expiration period, the stock has gone to $13.00 or greater, the stock will most likely be called against the $13 strike option the trader wrote. He will have to exercise his $13.50 strike option and his loss on the write contract will be ($50 - $21) = $29 plus commissions loss for the entire transaction. So, there is limited risk for the vertical spread.

A similar transaction could be done if the trader expects the stock to increase in value. It would then be called a "Bull Put Spread". In this case the trader might short the $13.50 strike put, and long the $13 put for a net credit of $30 less commissions per contract on initiation. Now as the stock increases above $13.50, the value of the short put declines and it is not executed. If the stock goes down, then the net loss for the transaction will be limited to ($50 - $30) = $20 per contract plus commissions.

So again, there is limited loss for the transaction. One word of advice: Before initiating either of the above options you should contact your broker and explain your intention to make sure the broker agrees with your transaction and will not be alarmed when you write the short options.

Option Chain for General Electric Company (GE)

Calls	Last	Chg	Bid	Ask	Vol	Open Int	Root	Strike	Puts	Last	Chg	Bid	Ask	Vol	Open Int
Aug 03, 2018	1.26		1.12	1.14	0	13	GE	12	Aug 03, 2018	0.25	0.03	0.25	0.27	19	178
Aug 03, 2018	0.81	-0.08	0.78	0.80	3	44	GE	12.5	Aug 03, 2018	0.39	0.05	0.40	0.42	8	104
Aug 03, 2018	0.53	-0.05	0.51	0.53	11	236	GE	13	Aug 03, 2018	0.63	0.09	0.62	0.65	30	6
Aug 03, 2018	0.32	-0.05	0.31	0.33	74	875	GE	13.5	Aug 03, 2018	0.93	0.04	0.93	0.95	1	61

Table 8, Option Chain for GE stock.

Data like the above can be obtained from the NASDAQ, the CBOE and others:

https://www.nasdaq.com/quotes/real-time.aspx

http://www.cboe.com/delayedquote/quote-table

6.7 Butterflies and Other Endangered Species

There are some multiple options positions that traders use to obtain profits in stable markets. They have various names but the common ones are the Butterfly, the Iron Butterfly, and the Condor. I do not recommend these because the stock markets have become very volatile recently and also because of the complexity of the positions and relatively high commission costs for the transactions.

In the case of butterflies and the other similar constructs, it is important to note that the trader should use only those options that are European style to protect against early assignment by the short option owner. European style options are not available for equities but only for certain index funds. The newer index funds are mostly European style. Here are some index funds that are popular on major indices: SPX (S&P 500). NDAQ (NASDAQ), RUT (Russell 2000), and DJX (Dow Jones 30.)

6.7.1 The Butterfly

The butterfly option trading method is set up to take advantage of a stable market over a certain period of time. The time period of the option is the time to expiration, or more precisely the time left from the time the position is initiated to the time the position expires. The objective is to have a long enough expiration to make a profit from the short positions, but not too long to risk moving into a loss situation. The trader must carefully evaluate how likely it is that the market is stable enough to allow him or her to make a profit for the expiration time he has selected (all of the options in the construct should expire at the same time.)

We will construct a butterfly position on the NDAQ (NASDAQ.) See the table below for July 20 expiration options.

Calls	Last	Chg	Bid	Ask	Vol	Open Int	Root	Strike	Puts	Last	Chg	Bid	Ask
Jul 20, 2018	7.45	-2.38	7.60	8.00	3	10	NDAQ	85	Jul 20, 2018	0.25		0.15	0.35
Jul 20, 2018	7.28		5.40	5.70	0	7	NDAQ	87.5	Jul 20, 2018	0.60		0.35	0.50
Jul 20, 2018	3.40		3.30	3.50	3	35	NDAQ	90	Jul 20, 2018	0.80	-0.25	0.75	0.90
Jul 20, 2018	1.75	0.15	1.65	1.85	1	167	NDAQ	92.5	Jul 20, 2018	1.90		1.55	1.70
Jul 20, 2018	0.55		0.65	0.75	0	152	NDAQ	95	Jul 20, 2018	3.30		3.00	3.30
Jul 20, 2018	0.21	0.06	0.15	0.30	2	615	NDAQ	97.5	Jul 20, 2018	4.50		5.00	5.30
Jul 20, 2018	0.05			0.10	0	72	NDAQ	100	Jul 20, 2018	5.59		7.40	8.20

Table 9, Option Chain for the NASDAQ Index (NDAQ)

To construct the butterfly from the above data we will initiate the following positions with dollar amounts per contract (multiply by 100 to get total price of the 100 shares in one contract.) Note that when buying an option, you will have to pay the "ask" price, and when you sell an option, you will only get the "bid" price.

Long 20 July 97.5 strike call $0.30
Short 20 July 92.5 strike call $1.65
Long 20 July 87.5 strike put $0.50
Short 20 July 92.5 strike put $1.55

On initiating the above position, we will have a credit of $3.20 or $320, and a debit of $0.80 or $80, for a net credit of $240 per contract less commissions. The $240 less commissions is also the maximum profit for the transaction.

The maximum loss will be the difference between the ATM (at the money) price of $92.5 and the end points of 87.5 and 97.5, which is $500 in the above construct, less the initial credit of $240, or $260 plus commissions. Note that the risk can easily be evaluated against the money loss / profit which is 1.083, or the risk is a little greater than one for the trade (This would ordinarily be acceptable to a trader.)

The credit will be in our account the same day the transaction is initiated (Make sure you talk to your broker before you do a butterfly in case he has any problem with you doing the trade.)

Below is a chart of the profit and loss vs. the stock price for the above transaction.

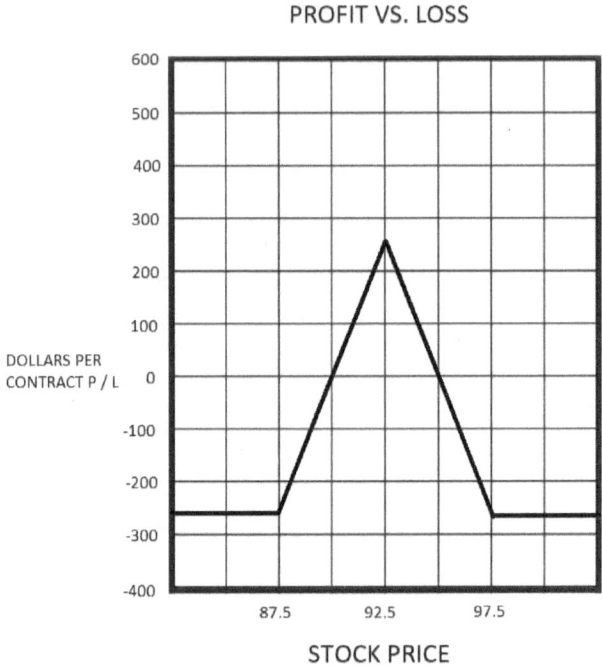

Fig. 13, A "Butterfly" option spread for the NASDAQ Index.

Note from the above chart that the maximum range of stock price for no loss is from $90 to $95, and that the profitable range for the butterfly described above is an even smaller range. This is the chief problem with the butterfly construct. Another problem with the above butterfly is that it is using options from a fairly volatile index, so a profit is unlikely and a loss is more likely. In the next section we will describe a better approach to butterfly trades with the "Iron Butterfly".

There are other types of butterflies, such as a short butterfly which depends on a volatile market for profit. I do not recommend short butterflies because of the high risk. We will however discuss the "Iron Butterfly" in the next section.

6.7.1.1 The Iron Butterfly

An improved butterfly is the Iron Butterfly which gives a much broader range of profitability and a greater chance of success, especially if it is set up with a stable market index, and even during a low volatility period for the index.

We will construct the iron butterfly using the S&P 500 index, SPX, using CBOE data (Chicago Board of Exchange):

http://www.cboe.com/delayedquote/quote-table

And data per the following option table:

Calls — JULY 2018 (EXPIRATION: 07/02)

Strike	Last	Net	Bid	Ask	Vol	Int
SPXW1802G2750-E	1.60	-0.40	1.45	1.65	228	1801
SPXW1802G2760-E	0.65	-0.45	0.55	0.70	96	1180

Puts — JULY 2018 (EXPIRATION: 07/02)

Strike	Last	Net	Bid	Ask	Vol	Int
SPXW1802S2640-E	2.70	-1.48	2.30	2.50	64	429
SPXW1802S2650-E	3.20	-3.10	3.10	3.30	230	1817

Table 10, Option chain for the S&P 500 Index (SPX).

The Iron Butterfly will now be constructed for a range of approximately 100 points to cover the current range of volatility for the year as the following:

Long 1 contract 18 July strike 2760   call $0.70
Short 1 contract 18 July strike 2750   call $1.45
Long 1 contract 18 July strike 2640   put $2.50

Short   1 contract 18   July   strike   2650   put $3.10

The net credit for this construct is $1.35 less commissions per contract. The profit if only one contract each is initiated, but in this case a trader might do 5 or 10 contracts for a larger total credit. If the index does not stay within the range of 2650 to 2750, a 100-point range, and falls totally out of the range of the construct, there is a $10 loss per contract plus commissions but adjusted for the credit of $1.35, or a worst-case loss of $8.65 per contract plus commissions.

On the basis of money loss / profit, the risk of this trade would compute to approximately 6.4. If 10 contracts were bought with a credit of $1355, it should be noted that is the Iron butterfly falls out of either the top or bottom range. A worst-case loss of $6400 could result! However, the construct covered a very wide range of index prices over a fairly short period of time to expiration, so the risk is not great, baring a major decline in the market.

The trader must carefully evaluate the volatility of the index he is trading with in the time period he is trading, and the risk of a major market downward of upward move. Once the position is initiated there is no remedy to "fix" it later due to the fact that the options cannot be exercised until the end of the expiration period.

Below is the profit or loss chart for the S&P 500 Iron Butterfly.

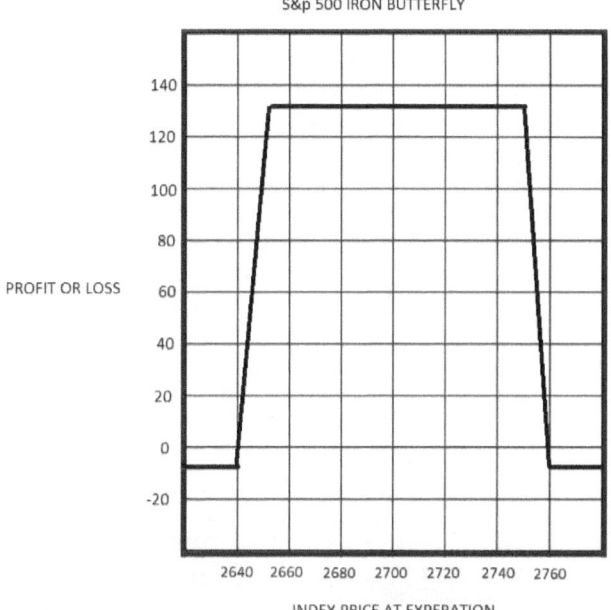

Fig. 14, An "Iron Butterfly" option spread for the S&P 500 Index (SPX).

6.7.1.2 The Condor

There are many kinds of "Condors" in option trading. There is a long condor, there is a short condor, and a condor look-alike construct called a "Combo". Here we will discuss the traditional condor which combines long and short options to make a profit with a stable market condition. This kind of condor has the controlled risk of backing up the short positions with long positions like the butterflies described above to achieve a construct that is designed to profit as long as the stock (index) stays within a given range.

To construct the traditional condor, we will write what is called a short "combination" or "combo" with a short put close to the low side of the range and a short call at the high side of the range. Then to limit risk we will buy a long put at the low side of the range, and a long call at the high side of the range.

In the month of June, the RUT (index for the Russell 2000), moved over the range of 1643 to 1707 and ended at approximately 1643, a range of 64 points. We will build our condor to range from about 1620 to 1670 to have a range of +, - 25 approximately points from the current price of 1643. Because the time to expiration of our options is only 6 days, we are allowing approximately 4 points change per day in one direction before the condor becomes unprofitable. Normally we would not have a unidirectional movement in the index, but the index usually fluctuates up and down from day-to-day, so this condor is fairly conservative.

Calls   JULY 2018 (EXPIRATION: 07/06)

RUTW1806G1620-E	28.98	+2.36	27.90	31.50	6	22
RUTW1806G1625-E	27.37	+5.23	24.30	27.60	1	19
RUTW1808G1685-E	3.83	-1.99	3.60	4.40	69	198
RUTW1806G1670-E	2.65	-2.32	2.50	3.20	66	224
RUTW1806G1690-E	0.62	-0.66	0.40	0.80	111	342

Puts   JULY 2018 (EXPIRATION: 07/06)

RUTW1806S1620-E	5.30	-1.59	4.70	5.50	404	318
RUTW1806S1625-E	6.49	-1.79	5.70	6.60	40	356
RUTW1806S1665-E	21.09	-3.82	22.60	26.20	22	81
RUTW1806S1670-E	25.22	-3.80	26.20	30.20	46	184
RUTW1806S1590-E	1.58	-1.32	1.35	1.80	94	211

Table 11, Option chain for the Russell 2000 Index (RUT).

The our first construct is:

Short 1 contract 6 July 1665 strike call $3.60
Short 1 contract 6 July 1625 strike put $5.70
Long 1 contract 6 July   1670 strike call $3.20
Long 1 contract 6 July   1620 strike put $5.50

The credit for the transaction is $60 per contract less commissions. The worst-case loss is $500 per contract.

Now the profit does not seem like a lot of money, and you could actually owe the broker money with the above trade, especially if you have a full-service broker.

But suppose you could do 20 contracts a week for 20 weeks of the year. The 20 contracts make the commissions small compared to the $1200 that 20 contracts would yield for a credit on each condor like the above. Your total per year would be 20 X 60 X 50 = $60,000 less commissions (with two weeks of vacation also.)

If you allowed more points spread between the highest and lowest long contracts and the short contracts, the credit would be even higher (but the risk be higher too.) Let's consider another example where we spread the wings of the condor quite a bit. Again, we use the same two short contracts:

Short 1 contract 6 July 1665 strike call $3.60
Short 1 contract 6 July 1625 strike put $5.70

But now we extend the wings (long contract points spreads) as:

Long 1 contract 6 July 1690 strike call $0.30
Long 1 contract 6 July 1590 strike put $1.80

Now the net credit is $7.20 per contract, or $720 for only 1 contract! So, what is the disadvantage? Is this too good to be true? The problem is that the risk has gone up from $440 per contract plus commissions to $2780 per contract worst case plus commissions.

So always remember high return on an investment is usually accompanied by higher risk. Also remember that the European style options that we use for butterflies and condors cannot not be closed prior to expiration in order to cut losses!

In the next section we will discuss the use of American style options to do options trades using "calendar spreads" also known as time spreads.

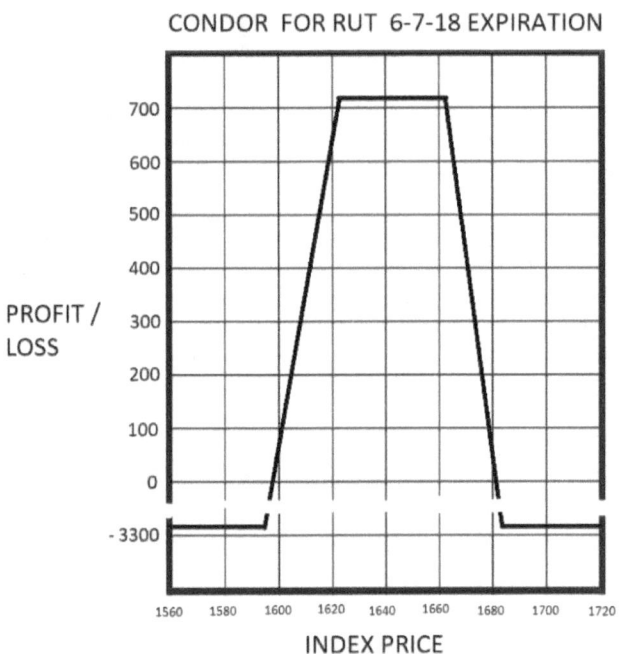

Fig. 15, A "Condor" option spread for the Russell 2000 Index (RUT)

6.7.2 Calendar Spreads

Calendar spreads, also known as time spreads are options trades with limited risk that are designed to return profits in stable markets. For this kind of trade, we desire a stable market for the stock that we trade options with. We will also use equities for which American style options apply.

Let's take an example of a calendar spread for Walmart stock. We will go long 1 contract on WMT for a December 21 expiration at a strike of $80 for a $845 debit, and short 1 contract on WMT for July 27 at a strike of 89 for a credit of $41 per contract. See the tables below.

Calls for December 21, 2018

Contract Name	Last Trade Date	Strike	Last Price	Bid	Ask
WMT181221C00055000	2018-05-30 3:31PM EDT	55.00	29.50	27.85	28.80
WMT181221C00060000	2018-05-11 11:54PM EDT	60.00	22.89	22.55	24.80
WMT181221C00065000	2018-06-29 11:58PM EDT	65.00	21.25	21.00	22.00
WMT181221C00070000	2018-05-14 2:48PM EDT	70.00	16.36	15.70	16.30
WMT181221C00075000	2018-05-11 11:54PM EDT	75.00	11.30	11.10	11.35
WMT181221C00077500	2018-06-27 11:48AM EDT	77.50	11.64	11.20	11.35
➡ WMT181221C00080000	2018-06-29 3:38PM EDT	80.00	8.60	8.20	8.45
WMT181221C00082500	2018-06-27 3:28PM EDT	82.50	7.60	6.50	6.75

Calls for July 27, 2018

Contract Name	Last Trade Date	Strike	Last Price	Bid	Ask
WMT180727C00088500	2018-06-28 10:19AM EDT	88.50	1.02	0.52	0.56
➡ WMT180727C00089000	2018-06-29 3:06PM EDT	89.00	0.48	0.41	0.45
WMT180727C00089500	2018-06-29 11:23AM EDT	89.50	0.43	0.32	0.36

Table 12, Option chain for Walmart Stock.

The December 21 80 strike call is deep ITM (in the money) and the July 27 89 strike call is OTM (out of the money.)

Now during the month of July there are two possibilities.

1. The OTM call is not executed because the price of the stock does not exceed $89. In this case the trader keeps the $41 credit less commissions for the

month, and then can initiate a new option write again using his long $80 call as backup against loss.

2. The stock does exceed $89 and the short call is executed by the owner. The trader must exercise his long $80 call and receives 100 shares of stock for $80 per share. He then immediately transfers the 100 shares of stock to the owner of the option and he receives $89 for each share of stock. The trader has made $9 per share less commissions for his stock option exercise plus the $41 for his option write less his $845 debit on the long call and less commissions. So, he is left with a credit of $96 less commissions. The trader has chosen the correct strikes on the stock so that the trader makes a profit whether he is called on his short position or not.

3. If the trader executes 10 contracts then we can multiply his profits under the two possibilities above as $410 and $960 with his original long call at $8450 cost. This kind of a trade makes more sense for his time and risk.

What is the risk of the position? One risk is that the stock declines so much that his long call drops to an OTM (out of the money) state. In this case the broker will likely call the trader and ask for more money to back up the long option position. His accounting people get nervous and put pressure on the broker. Of course. this is really not needed because your long option still tops the original short option.

The real risk is that your long option loses its value if the stock drops significantly in price, and you have a big loss on your long call. Ideally you want your long option to keep its value or even increase in value so you can continue to write short term calls against it or even execute it and take your profit on the long call.

A normal condition is that your long call decays in value as the call nears its expiration date. So, you need to periodically close out your long position and buy a new long call. You can also buy calls with longer expiration dates so that you do not have to close out and re-buy your long call.

The longer the time to expiration, the more expensive the call is because there is more time for the stock to increase in value. If the price of the stock goes up significantly you could have a substantial gain on your long call that you can profit on. But of course, the short call must expire first or be closed out before you can sell your long call, or call the stock against your long call.

7.0 Appendix

1. Free Stock Screeners

Finviz.com

Yahoo.com

Stockfetcher.com

Chartmill.com

Stockrover.com

Finance.zacks.com

2. Stock Analysts / Services

Seekingalpha.com

Themotleyfool.com

Investopedia.com

Marketwatch.com

Thestreet.com (Jim Cramer)

Bloomberg.com

Marketbeat.com

Finance.zacks.com